HOPE in the Storms

People have called this book...

'Inspiring'

'Encouraging'

'Hopeful'

'Open and Honest'

'Vulnerable'

'Raw'

'Authentic'

'Transparent'

HOPE in the Storms

When faith can move mountains

CHANTAL GIORGINI

Hope in the Storms
Published by Chantal Giorgini
with Castle Publishing Ltd

© 2021 Chantal Giorgini

ISBN 978-0-646-84673-6 (Softcover)
ISBN 978-0-646-84674-3 (ePUB)
ISBN 978-0-646-84675-0 (Kindle)

Editing:
Sally Webster

Production & Typesetting:
Lizelle Windon & Andrew Killick
Castle Publishing Services
www.castlepublishing.co.nz

Cover Design:
Adrian Daly

All Scripture quotations,
unless otherwise indicated, are taken from
the Holy Bible, New International Version®, NIV®.
Copyright ©1973, 1978, 1984, 2011 by Biblica, Inc.™
Used by permission of Zondervan.
All rights reserved worldwide.

ALL RIGHTS RESERVED

No part of this publication may be reproduced,
stored in a retrieval system, or transmitted
in any form or by any means, electronic, mechanical,
photocopying, recording or otherwise,
without prior written permission from the author.

Contents

Introduction		7
1.	Why Me?	9
2.	Finding Strength in Your Storms	15
3.	Stolen Identity	23
4.	Death is Not the Answer	33
5.	Standing Strong in Your Singleness	45
6.	Two Years Too Long	57
7.	Double Blessing	65
8.	Taken Too Soon	75
9.	There is Always a Rainbow After the Storm	87
10.	Birthday Surprise	105
11.	The Aftermath	117
12.	When Your Storms Become a Shadow	125
13.	Miracles Do Happen	139
14.	Life Leeches	155
15.	Finding Joy in the Negatives	163
16.	Incurable Does Not Mean Final	173
17.	Anchored Hope	185
About the Author		193

Introduction

Dear Readers,

I remember coming home from a seminar in July 2015 and telling my parents that I was going to write a book about my life, about how keeping hope in God had pulled me through many storms. My parents were so supportive, and encouraged me to accomplish this goal. I attended my first book-writing course in September 2015, where I learnt, amongst other things, how to understand my target audience and speak to my readers.

Throughout my life I have encountered physical storms. So much so that it felt entirely normal – yet I was aware that they were continually happening to me, and not to the same extent to others around me. Even as I was writing this book, they continued presenting themselves.

About three weeks into starting my book, I had to face one of the biggest storms of my young life – a cancer scare. I couldn't believe the timing. My mind immediately became clouded, and all I could think were negative thoughts of how God couldn't control *this* one. Cancer became the dominant factor in my life. It made me think, 'How can I write a book on teaching others how to keep their faith alive during a storm, when in my own current storm I can barely believe how big my God is?' I never thought I would actually finish writing this book, being so challenged by my own words. I never thought I would become an author, and be a voice for other people. But instead of being capsized by this latest terrifying storm, I decided to keep writing in order to encourage others and show that it *is* possible to come out the other side safe and sound. It *is* possible to hold on to hope when you are at the end of your rope. *It is possible to get back up again.*

So, instead of giving up on writing, I simply added an extra chapter to my book – showing the specific challenges I went through during this time, and explaining how I overcame them, just like I did in all the other storms. Writing this book did not make me exempt from any more challenges. Rather it made me realise that God was double the size of my storm. I put all my hope in Him, and He never let me down once. He never has and He never will. He is *always* faithful. He was there for me all the time, quietly working behind the scenes.

I faced a lot of opposition in writing this book. But I said to God: 'It doesn't matter if I lose friends over this, or if I encounter another severe storm, or if I lose everything because of it, I will still publish this book and bless people with my story.'

My aim in writing is not to elicit sympathy, but for you to be blessed and encouraged by these words and stories. My prayer is that it will restore hope and draw you closer to God. Remember, He is your Father in Heaven and He loves you so much. He wants an amazing future for you, one that will enrich and prosper you. My hope is that you will share this book with your family and friends, and thereby encourage them too.

Chantal

Chapter 1
WHY ME?

'For I know the plans I have for you,' declares the Lord, 'plans to prosper you and not to harm you, plans to give you hope and a future.'

Jeremiah 29:11

Target acquired. Ready. Aim. Fire. This was how I used to think about my life. I felt as though I had a huge target painted on my back, and that I was waiting for someone or something to take aim at me. I used to think that I had been born accident-prone. As a result, I was always wondering what would happen next. What might hurt me now? What sickness was waiting around the corner for me? One by one the physical challenges restricted me. As soon as one finished, the next would not be too far away. It felt like an unending domino effect in my life.

Sometimes I felt like the whole world was against me. I saw other people succeeding in life, whereas I always felt restricted. I felt I was living in a bubble, watching other people live their lives, and I always ended up in pain.

One word that I disliked yet very often heard was 'always'. People would say to me, 'You're *always* sick,' or 'You're *always* injured.' Even though it hurt hearing this, I realised there was some truth to it. There *was* always something physically wrong with me. It was so frustrating to be *always* sick in bed, or *always* missing out on the fun because of the pain I was suffering and the restrictions that came with being injured. It never felt fair.

I *always* seemed to have major medical problems. I would have done anything to instead experience a minor injury such as a sprained ankle or some other minor condition. Whenever I went to the doctors my parents would have to brace themselves because I so often came back with a severe and rare diagnosis, most of which led to the worst-case scenario of needing surgery.

When I was in kindergarten at primary school, a boy who didn't like me decided to sharpen a lead pencil and stick it in my spine. I don't remember it all too well because I was so young at the time, but I specifically recall being placed in an ambulance and being taken to hospital. Then later, when I was in high school, I somehow managed to sit on a rusty needle, which led to my receiving a tetanus shot. It just felt crazy that, no matter where I went or what I did or where I sat, I always ended up in some sort of pain.

All through my life physical illness followed me. It was like a shadow that wouldn't leave me. When I was in primary school I was so often either in the sickbay or being picked up by my mum. My primary school knew me as the 'sick' kid. I wanted to remove that label when I moved to high school. However, there too physical storms followed me into my teen years, and my friends would often see me sick, injured or on crutches.

Even at my church I felt I was labelled accident-prone. When bad things happened to me no one really reacted because it seemed entirely normal for me. Seeing me walk through the church doors on crutches, nobody seemed surprised. They would say to me, 'What have you done now?'

Everywhere I went I felt that the storm was close behind me, like a twister that was on my tail, ready to swallow me up. And I disliked that feeling. I often imagined moving to different places and taking on a new identity so I wouldn't be known as the 'sick' kid anymore. There has hardly been any time in my life, even up to now, when I have been free from physical pain, either major or minor.

In every storm I went through, the first question I would ask God was: 'Why me?' I would see other people growing, but I would feel that I was stuck in the same place all the time. It got to the point where I actually *expected* something bad to happen to me. It felt routine. It felt normal. I had labelled my personality with sickness to such an extent that, on the very rare occasion when I was pain free, I actually felt empty.

I would see other people free from sickness, able to live their lives without physical pain, and compare myself to them. I was either sitting down because standing was too painful, or standing up because sitting was too painful – either way I felt like I just couldn't win in life. I felt restricted and defeated.

If you, like me, feel you have a target on your back, then I can tell you how I overcame this. I'm not promising that you will never again encounter storms, because unfortunately our bodies grow more fragile as we age, and there will still be lots of challenges on your path. We are not exempt from suffering because we are Christians. But it is our *attitude* that matters most. Easier said than done, right?

Do you look at your glass as half full or half empty? Your answer will determine your attitude throughout your storm.

I learnt through all that I suffered to trust God *through* every storm. I also learnt to smile through every storm because I knew God had my back. I eventually figured out that there is no such thing as having a target on your back. But there *is* such a thing as the devil, and he wants to make you think that you are a target. He wants you to think that God doesn't love you, and that God is punishing you with these storms.

The devil's role is to steal your joy, kill your fun, control your thoughts and destroy your faith in God. The devil wants your faith. That's all he's after, because once he has that, he has everything he wants.

What I found helpful was not letting the storm put a stop sign in my life. If I loved singing and I couldn't stand, then I would sit and sing. If I wanted to dance and I couldn't stand up, I would dance sitting down in my chair. I wouldn't let my storms capsize my lifeboat. Yes, I still felt restricted in some things, but I tried to remain positive. I tried to have fun despite my difficulties. I tried to enjoy life no matter the pain I was feeling. Enjoying and appreciating life is what mattered.

My *faith in God* played a huge part of getting me through my storms. **What do I mean by 'faith in God'?**

- Knowing that God was by my side the entire way – this helped me to persevere.
- Knowing that God had my future in His hands so I could walk by faith, not by sight.
- Knowing that God was proud of me and that He was cheering for me.

- Knowing that I would not get burnt in the fire or be overtaken by the waves because that was God's promise to me.
- Knowing that I had an eternal inheritance in Heaven when my time on earth was over.
- Knowing that God was always accessible and that He always heard my prayers.
- Knowing that, if I didn't have enough strength to push through certain storms in my life, God would carry me in His arms and be my strength.

What you speak over your life is powerful. Words have power. You can either speak words of life or words of death over your situation. If you believe that you have a target on your back, then you will be stuck in the same trap of lies and deceit that I was in. If you find yourself in this place, start to speak words of *life* over yourself. God has not given you these disasters. He wants you to have a great and prosperous life.

So, block out all the lies of the enemy and listen only to the one voice that will direct your path in the way of life. Listen to the voice of Truth. Then He will be by your side encouraging you throughout your journey and giving you strength when you need it. Think of it as a race that you are running with God waiting on the sideline to cheer you on and at the finishing line to celebrate with you. He wants to see you finish the race.

LET'S SAY A PRAYER

Lord, I pray that you will help me believe that I do not have a target on my back. Lord, help me to value myself. Help me to keep my hope alive in you. In your name, I believe that this target is lifted off my life and will never return. Lord, I believe you have plans to help me prosper and give me a bright future. I want to see that happen. So, Lord, please lift all burdens off me, and remove all thoughts from the devil. He has no control over my life. Lord, I give *you* control over all my thoughts. When storms come my way, help me to have faith in you and to keep running this race with the strength and perseverance that you have given me. I pray all of this in Jesus' name. Amen.

CHAPTER REVIEW

- You do not have a target on your back.
- Your attitude will determine how you react to your storm.
- Don't let your storm put a STOP sign in your life.
- Put your faith in God because He will never let you down.
- Speak words of positivity over your life.
- Keep running your race with perseverance.

Chapter 2
FINDING STRENGTH IN YOUR STORMS

> 'So do not fear, for I am with you; do not be dismayed, for I am your God. I will strengthen you and help you; I will uphold you with my righteous right hand.'
>
> Isaiah 41:10

There was one positive thing about going through so many storms in my life – through them I found my true strength, and learned how much I could really handle. But it wasn't my own strength. It was the strength of God that got me through every difficulty. Without Him, I don't know if I would be here right now. He has brought me through so many challenges, and I am extremely thankful to Him for doing so. It was my faith in God that kept me strong all these years. And my hope in Him kept me anchored in His promises.

Whilst growing up I was considered 'accident-prone', and this allowed people to see my ability to bounce back even stronger than I had been before. In my church youth group I was known as being spiritually and emotionally strong – not only did *they* see me in this light, but I believed it myself! Even at home I was referred to as the 'rock' of the family. They would depend on me and turn to me during times of trouble – because they knew I could not only handle my own storms but also help them through theirs. I can look back on every storm I have ever faced, and thank God for getting me through each one successfully. Sometimes I would actually thank Him *for* the storm that I had just encountered. Sounds weird, right? Thanking God for the very storm that put you through so much pain? But, surprisingly, every storm you go through (whether it be physical, emotional or spiritual) makes your *faith in God* bolder. It also makes you look back on previous storms and compare how well you coped. Soon you realise that your strength for the next storm will be built on the 'success' of your handling of all those past ones.

I once had an agonising ankle injury that persisted for two whole years (I talk in more detail about this in Chapter 6). So, when the next comparatively minor storm came along, I was able to look at it and say, 'If I was able to get through those two agonising years, I can get through anything.' I even asked myself, 'If I had to go through everything I have faced so far *again*, would I willingly do it?' My answer was and still is, 'Yes.' I never could have guessed that I would end up saying that!

When you are in the middle of a storm, it's never easy to foresee a positive outcome. But after you have come through it successfully, you realise how much you have changed. There's new strength and growth. You realise that God will never give you anything that you can't handle – this is His promise in the Bible (see 1 Corinthians 10:13). No matter what you may have to encounter, He will give you both the strength and the perseverance to push through and reach the finishing line successfully. *All you have to do is to ask Him to help you.* Remember, after the storm has passed a rainbow appears, bringing joy and hope – a reminder of God's promises to us.

Have you *thanked* God for the storms in your life? I know it sounds weird to thank Him for the heartache or pain that you are experiencing. But God can make *everything* beautiful in His own time. You may not be able to thank Him straight away, because perhaps the pain is still fresh and raw. That is fine. God has created us with emotions, and it is normal to feel that way. Eventually, as the days and months go by, you will find yourself getting stronger, and your heart will start to heal. Then you will be able to thank Him for getting you through it. You will know yourself as both a survivor and a warrior. You will be standing on your own two feet again. And you will realise that you didn't succeed alone – God was by your side the entire time. Remember, He will never leave you nor forsake you. There is no reason to fear, because God is with you always.

Finding strength in your storms can be difficult, and it is so easy to allow yourself to wallow in your misery. Trust me, I know what that feels like. I remember times when the pain became too much, when I didn't even want to get out of bed – I thought I had reached the end of my ability to go on. You probably know how that feels. What you need to remember when you reach that low point is that God is *still* writing your story. *He* holds the pen. *He* is in control. *Let* Him continue writing. You just be His masterpiece, as He has called you to be. He has taught us to pray to Him and ask for His help.

How amazing it is to know that, no matter what situation you are in, God will uphold you with His righteous hand, *if you ask Him*. To know that He is there to support you and lift you up. I see an analogy in weightlifting, with God being the 'spotter'. In weight training, spotting is the act of supporting another person during an exercise, with the emphasis on allowing them to lift or 'push' more than they would normally handle. This is exactly what God does in our lives. Whenever we embark on a new journey or on something that He has called us to do, He is spotting us – firstly by making sure we are supported and safe, and secondly by encouraging us to push ourselves further and go that extra mile. But we have to remember to pray and ask for that help.

When you pray for strength, God is not instantly going to make you strong and fearless. It doesn't work like that. He will give you opportunities in which you can choose either to be strong or fearful. We should not do anything in our own strength, but rather rely on God's strength. *He* is our pillar of strength. Even when we cannot go on any longer and feel we have exhausted our supply of energy, He can hold us up and fight our battles for us. All we need to do is pray.

> **The Lord is my strength and shield. I trust him with all my heart. He helps me, and my heart is filled with joy. I burst out in songs of thanksgiving.**
> **Psalm 28:7 NLT**

This verse helps us understand that God is there to help us and that He is our Father. What exactly is a father's role? It is to protect and provide for his children, and to nurture them. A good father is someone who is selfless, and who puts himself 'out there' to keep his children safe. Just so with our heavenly Father – no matter what comes our way, He will protect and shield us, and help us in times of need. The Lord is *your* heavenly Father. He will protect you and provide for you. So why wouldn't *you* respond with thanksgiving?

Over the years I have come to realise that becoming

strong is a journey. It doesn't happen overnight, but rather gradually. It is like exercising – in the beginning you start off really slowly, and your body feels much pain. However, if you are consistent, your body starts to adapt to the pain and your muscles start developing. You gradually become fitter and you can push yourself more and more.

As you go through various storms in life, you will find that you start off reacting really fearfully. But as you continue to face them, you will gradually build up courage and faith, and you will become stronger and bolder in your ministry and your day-to-day life.

When facing the challenges and traumas of life, a support network is essential. Make sure you have people around you who understand you and know how best to show their love. There are five so-called 'love languages', which describe the main avenues by which people feel appreciated and loved. They are: physical touch, words of affirmation, gift-giving, acts of service and quality time. Each of us is motivated by one or two of these languages more than by the others. My personal love language is 'words of affirmation'. During the stormy seasons, my friends sent me cards filled with encouraging Bible verses and personal comments. Others spoke to me over the phone or sent messages reminding me that I was strong and that I could get through the crisis. These affirming words helped me so much, and helped me to stay positive.

Other people will never 'understand' exactly what you are going through, but they will be able to empathise with you. My family has seen me go through so much in my life. It really affected them too, more especially because most of the time they felt helpless in being able to make things better for me. And in this way they shared in my suffering.

Others cannot *feel* your pain the way you do, but they can nevertheless see and share in your suffering. In this way you are never alone. There may be nothing others can do except pray for you and encourage you to keep persevering. And sometimes that might be all you need in order to persevere. I remember one night finding my mum crying in the lounge, and when I asked her what was wrong, she replied, 'It's not fair. Why are bad things always happening to you? I don't like seeing you like this.' That's when it really hit me that she too was suffering my pain. I had never thought about it before.

Your situation *can* change, based on your attitude. You can either sit around and mope, or you can get back up and help others. If you sit around miserably you will miss out on opportunities. Time will move by and you will not be moving with it.

You may be going through something right now where you feel alone and weak. Remember that your family and friends see what you are going through and experience this with you. Go through this situation with them by your side, encouraging and helping you. Their support and prayers might just be the tools needed in assisting you in moving forward.

Not everyone has someone to support them. Some of you are going through your storm alone. But remember – you are never alone! If you build your life on the foundation of other people's help and support, you will inevitably be disappointed. But if you build your life with Jesus Christ as your foundation, He will never let you down. You will never fall. Christ is the unshakeable firm foundation. Ask Him to help you. And ask Him to give you a friend who will be there to love and support you.

LET'S SAY A PRAYER

Lord, I pray for the storm that I am currently dealing with. It is really difficult, and I don't see a way out. Yet I know that you are still writing my story, and that it is not over yet. As I look to you, I pray that you will help me make it through this storm. Thank you for upholding and supporting me throughout this trial. Thank you that this storm is making me stronger. Help me to continue to find strength in you. Help me to keep persevering and running this race with you. Not only do I have you, Lord, but also those people you have brought into my life to support and encourage me. I am so blessed by them. I thank you for all of this, Jesus. Amen.

CHAPTER REVIEW

- You cannot succeed in your own strength – you need God's strength.
- Learn to thank God for the storms you go through.
- Each new storm makes you stronger than before.
- God will never leave you nor forsake you.
- Your story hasn't ended yet – God is still writing it.
- Make sure that you have the right support around you.

Chapter 3
STOLEN IDENTITY

As iron sharpens iron, so one person sharpens another.

Proverbs 27:17

When I was 12 years old and in my last year of primary school, I was chosen to be School Captain. This meant that I was often out of class attending meetings or organising events, which resulted in my schoolwork falling behind. So my Year 6 teacher kindly offered me one-on-one tutoring sessions after school, when everyone else had gone home. My parents were fine with this, thinking it would help me catch up.

However, this teacher used his position and dominant nature to take advantage of me. He would corner me in the classroom and touch me inappropriately through my clothing, calling it a 'friendly pat'. I hated what he was doing to me, and I was confused and afraid. Nowadays children of that age know about abuse, but it was less talked about at that time, and I didn't understand what was happening.

Even though he made me feel very uncomfortable and afraid, I kept on putting up with it. I just couldn't speak up, even though I knew it was wrong. I was afraid of telling my parents, so I was forced into silence. I felt trapped, with no escape. I eventually felt I was at the end of my tether.

Then one day it became too much for me, and I remember running home in tears and explaining everything to my parents. They immediately contacted the principal and informed her of what was going on, and the teacher was given a warning. That was all, and he was allowed to continue teaching there after I left. Even more incredibly, I still had to be in his class for the rest of the year. I couldn't transfer to another one because there was only one class per grade. All I could do was try to stay away from him as much as possible. It was a very uncomfortable situation, and every day for the rest of that year was hell for me. I couldn't wait to go up to high school the next year.

The whole experience left me feeling like a part of me had been taken away. I felt like a puzzle that was missing some of its pieces. I wasn't a complete picture anymore. I had lost part of my identity. I remember being so angry with God, and asking Him, 'Why did that happen to me? Why did he target *me* out of the whole class?' I thought God was punishing me for something, and just couldn't understand why. I had always been a 'good' girl. I stayed out of trouble, made good choices and hung out with the right crowd. I had been considered responsible enough to be given the role of School Captain, because teachers saw leadership potential in me. Consequently, I couldn't comprehend why this abuse had happened to me.

I remember turning away from God. I stopped going to church. I put my Bible in my drawer, so I didn't have to look at it. I made excuses to my friends for not attending youth meetings. I didn't want anything more to do with church or God at that point. I felt like He didn't love me anymore.

That teacher had stolen my identity and, as a result, I didn't feel like a teenager anymore. I had suddenly grown up very quickly. I matured early on because this experience – it forced me to be strong, socially aware and responsible at a young age. Even today people say that I act much older than I am.

At the same time I changed my name from Chantal to Chelle. When anyone called me Chantal, I was reminded of that vulnerable young girl who had lost her identity. When I was referred to as Chelle, I felt like a new person – a fun-loving, bubbly, crazy personality. People have always asked me why I don't like being called Chantal. I tell them that I just don't like the name. They couldn't guess the real reason for it.

Up to now I have kept much of this secret, so what I have written will probably shock my friends and family members. The name 'Chelle' represented the new personality I had created, one who didn't have to remember the abuse in her past. Chelle replaced Chantal's missing pieces, albeit temporarily. Although I didn't know it at the time, this *wasn't* what I needed. I really needed to invite *God* back into my life. He was the only one who could heal me. I thought that changing my name and creating a new identity would solve the problem. But it didn't.

HIGH SCHOOL SHADOW

For many people, starting high school can be a daunting experience. The first year is especially hard – finding new friends, fitting in and adapting to the new school environment with its new subjects and teachers. I thought that, now I had moved on, all the primary school trauma was finally behind me. Nobody in my high school knew about my past experiences, so I felt I could start again with a clean slate. I was both excited and relieved. Little did I know, things were far from over.

Unbeknown to me, a friend of mine back at my old primary school was going through exactly the same abuse with exactly the same teacher – only she, unlike me, reported it earlier. And this time it was followed up, not ignored.

I remember one lunchtime sitting around with my new friends. Suddenly the principal walked over with this girl from my primary school, who pointed me out. The principal then asked me to follow them back to her office. I had no idea what was going on, and fearfully and unknowingly followed. As we walked down the school corridors, the stares that we received on the way seemed endless. I hung my head so I didn't have to look at anyone. I felt ashamed, thinking I must have done something terribly wrong.

When we arrived at the office, my friend was escorted in and I was told to wait outside. There I was left, trying to think of any event that could have resulted in my being summoned to the principal's office. My mind was blank. I was a good student – I had never been in any trouble and had never had a detention. You can imagine my anxiety and confusion at being there.

The meeting inside didn't last long. When the girl came out she looked at me and said, 'That was weird,' and walked off. Then it was my turn. I took a deep breath as the principal ushered me into her office. On entering, I encountered a person I'd never seen before. He was holding a clipboard and some documents. As I scanned the room, I noticed a tape recorder on the table. He explained that he was a reporter, and asked permission to record my testimony of what had happened with my Year 6 teacher. I agreed. I felt like there was nothing else I could do.

I remember tearing up as I revisited those traumatic memories and brought them to back to life. It was not easy to share, but I was determined to be cooperative. To make matters worse, I had to talk about it in front of my new principal, whom I had only just met. I didn't want her to hear what had happened to me and label me because of it. I wanted a fresh start at my new school. But it was too late for that.

My past abuse felt like a shadow that was following me wherever I went. After I had answered all the questions, the reporter asked my permission to use the recording in court. I started to freak out. I didn't want to go to court; I was only 13 years old, and felt very afraid. I said 'yes' to using my testimony, but 'no' to appearing in court.

After that I remember running out and looking for my sister (who was in Year 10 at the time), But I couldn't find her. I wanted her to hug and comfort me. She knew my story, and how badly it had affected me. I didn't want to tell my new friends about any of it because I didn't want to be seen as a victim. I felt so dreadful. I felt like crying, screaming and throwing things. All I kept thinking was, 'This memory will never leave me. It will haunt me all my life.' It was like a leech that was sucking the life out of me. I had 'thrown salt' on it and tried to burn it out of my memory, but it would not die. It was a permanent part of me now.

Let's fast-forward a bit. The memory of the fear and abuse stayed with me for ten years without my knowing it. By that time I had unknowingly swept it under the carpet. I hadn't dealt with it at all. By then it had started affecting my relationships with boys – not only regarding dating, but even my ability to be in the same room as a guy. I couldn't trust them anymore, even ones that I had known for years. I imagined they all wanted to abuse me. I had put them all in the same box. The thought of sex scared me. The thought of marriage and being committed to one man for the rest of my life terrified me.

When boys walked towards me in the street, I would cross over to the other side. I finally realised how badly this was affecting my life when I became aware that I couldn't even look at my parents (or other couples) holding hands without having to walk away. That was when I knew it was time to deal with the trauma.

One day I invited my pastor and another leader to come to my office. They prayed for me for a long time. It was hard to let go of the fear and abuse – I had been holding onto it for so long that it had become part of me. It felt normal. But I knew it was finally time to let go. After much prayer, counselling and seeking the Holy Spirit, I was finally free. I even was able to forgive my teacher, not face-to-face but in my heart and out loud. I had started the session with my life fragmented, like puzzle pieces scattered all over the floor. By the end of it I felt whole – like a completed puzzle. My true identity had been restored.

At the same time I rekindled my relationship with God. When I opened my Bible again for the first time in ages, I read in Deuteronomy 31:6,

...He will never leave you nor forsake you.

I suddenly realised that during that whole time I had been pushing God away and turning my back on Him, He had been pursuing me, wanting a relationship with me. If you turn your back on a friend, even a very close one, there is little chance of ever having that friendship restored. But as soon as I turned back to God, He welcomed me with open arms. *What amazing love that is.*

I now was able to start trusting guys again. With the help of my counsellor, I even started dating. As a consequence, I entered into a serious relationship and as a result my belief in men fully restored. I shared my testimony of healing with others at my church and at work, and this helped many girls (especially those who had similarly been abused and were at a loss as to know how to overcome it) open up to me. When they saw my strong faith and hope in God despite all that had happened, they too wanted to know how they could be restored to wholeness.

I believe we go through experiences so that we can help, encourage and comfort others when they go through similar ones. Hence my writing this book.

> **Praise be to the God and Father of our Lord Jesus Christ, the Father of compassion and the God of all comfort, who comforts us in all our troubles, so that we can comfort those in any trouble with the comfort we ourselves receive from God.**
>
> 2 Corinthians 1:3-4

These verses tell us that when we go through difficult times, God is always there to comfort us. We are then able to show others the same comfort He has shown us.

I have learnt in my chaplaincy course that we will never completely understand what someone else is going through. Because they have a different personality and background, as well as different experiences, they will react and believe differently to us. However, we can still offer them empathy and support.

Many people have asked me how could I forgive that teacher. The answer is simple – I did so because I didn't want the abuse to hold me back anymore; I wanted freedom from that memory; I didn't want fear to rule or direct my life; I didn't want unforgiveness to weigh me down anymore. And that is what I received from God when I forgave my abuser. Forgiveness of others is the best thing you can give yourself. It doesn't excuse them from what they did, but it allows you to break those chains that have bound you to them, and to move forward in freedom of life.

As a result of what I have been through, I am now able to comfort and encourage others who have experienced abuse. I am able to offer them hope in their pain. *You can too.* Because of the challenges *you* have been through, you too can comfort others who are facing similar situations. You can tell them how God brought you through safely, and they will take encouragement in seeing how you are standing on your own feet again. You can be the voice of hope that they long to hear.

Referring to the verse at the start of this chapter, we read:

As iron sharpens iron, so one person sharpens another.

Proverbs 27:17

When two iron blades are rubbed together, each one becomes sharper and more effective than it previously was. So too have we been called to fellowship with others. If one falls, the other can help him or her up. As we sharpen or edify each other, we together become more effective.

If you have suffered any type of abuse (or know of someone who has), please do not let it continue afflicting you. You may have a partner who is physically, emotionally or verbally abusing you. This is not love. You need to seek the right help, and get yourself out of that situation. Then, once you are out, don't be tempted to sweep your feelings under the carpet. Go and see a professional counsellor, or get connected with a church and ask the pastors to pray for you. *Do not go through this alone.* Find the right support for your particular problem. Don't allow fear or depression to take over your life. Don't carry your burden around with you any longer. Receive the freedom that God makes available to you.

LET'S SAY A PRAYER

Lord, please help me to understand what true love is. It says in the Bible that *you* are love. Help me to experience this perfect love that removes all fear. Lord, help me to be forgiving towards others who have hurt me. And help them to understand that you love them and want to forgive them, regardless of what they have done. Lord, help me to let go of all my hurt and receive the freedom that you offer me. Help me to love others unconditionally, just like you love me. Lord, I pray that you will show me ways to comfort others with the same comfort that you have given me. Help me find my true identity in you. Use me as a vessel to help and edify others. I pray all of this in Jesus' name. Amen.

CHAPTER REVIEW

- Forgiveness does not excuse the other person from what they have done, but it frees you to move forward in life.
- Don't let fear rule your life.
- Use what you have been through in life to help, comfort and encourage others who have gone through similar experiences.
- Your true identity is in Jesus Christ alone.
- Even when you turn your back on God, He will pursue you and welcome you back with open arms.
- Let go of the past and receive the freedom of God.

Chapter 4
DEATH IS NOT THE ANSWER

> Do not be anxious about anything, but in every situation, by prayer and petition, with thanksgiving, present your requests to God. And the peace of God, which transcends all understanding, will guard your hearts and your minds in Christ Jesus.
>
> Philippians 4:6-7

People believe different things about what happens after death. Some believe that your earthly body stays in the ground and is at peace. Others believe in reincarnation, in which you come back to life on earth as a different being. I believe that there are only two eternal places where you can go after you die, either heaven or hell. No matter what you hear from others, hell is no party. The Bible says that it is a place of constant suffering, with weeping and gnashing of teeth. On the other hand it describes heaven as a beautiful place in which there is no pain or suffering but continual peace. Where do you want to spend eternity?

I'll be very honest with you, there were times when thoughts of suicide would come into my mind. It would be so easy to swerve my car in front of oncoming traffic. It felt like the easy way out, rather than constantly facing storms.

Rather than living with this or that chronic condition, or dealing with endless injuries and sicknesses, I would be free of pain. I would no longer feel that I was being constantly labelled by others. But, deeper than all those negative suicidal thoughts, was the belief that life was worth living and worth fighting for.

There is a great destiny awaiting those who believe in and follow Jesus Christ. Heaven and hell are real, and both are eternal. Many people don't think about what happens after death. They just want to escape the pain, loneliness and trauma of this earthly life. They don't think about the pain that their suicide will bring to family and friends left behind. Nor do they think about the good things they will miss out on once their troubles are past. All they focus on is escaping their current pain.

It was my faith in God that kept me alive. I cannot stress enough the importance of wearing your 'spiritual armour' when the enemy attacks. We need to remember who the real enemy is. It is not that family member or friend that has hurt you, nor even someone who has persecuted you. There is only one enemy, and his name is Satan. He wants to take your thoughts off the words of Jesus, steal your faith and use you as his puppet. Don't let him steal your peace.

> **Finally, be strong in the Lord and in his mighty power. Put on the full armour of God, so that you can take your stand against the devil's schemes. For our struggle is not against flesh and blood, but against the rulers, against the authorities, against the powers of this dark world and against the spiritual forces of evil in the heavenly realms. Therefore, put on the full**

armour of God, so that when the day of evil comes, you may be able to stand your ground, and after you have done everything, to stand. Stand firm then, with the belt of truth buckled around your waist, with the breastplate of righteousness in place, and with your feet fitted with the readiness that comes from the gospel of peace. In addition to all this, take up the shield of faith, with which you can extinguish all the flaming arrows of the evil one. Take the helmet of salvation and the sword of the Spirit, which is the word of God. And pray in the Spirit on all occasions with all kinds of prayers and requests. With this in mind, be alert and always keep on praying for all the Lord's people.

Ephesians 6:10-18

Soon after I had started my first job, I developed a huge crush on a boy. I was ready to tell him my feelings but, before I was able to, I found out that he liked another girl. At the time I remember being so crushed and hurt by this that I couldn't function properly. It was my first experience of being attracted to a boy and, coming relatively soon after the abuse, I didn't know how to handle it. I felt so rejected. I felt that my life wasn't worth living anymore, and that my world was slowly crumbling around me. I couldn't sleep or eat, and I felt numb. Pretty dramatic, right? It was my first serious 'crush' and I felt that if I couldn't have him, then I didn't want anyone at all.

Unfortunately, instead of dealing with these feelings or asking for help, I decided to take drastic measures. I was alone at the office one day, and once again I was obsessing over why this guy didn't like me. I kept thinking, 'I'm not pretty enough,' and 'I'm not worth anything.' I became very depressed – so low that I thought my life was not worth living without him.

I saw a pair of scissors on my desk, and hesitantly hovered them over my left arm. My hand started to shake. There was a battle raging in my mind. One voice was saying, 'Don't do it. There are plenty of other guys out there. Think about your family and your friends. This is stupid. Why are you going to harm or kill yourself over one guy?' The other, stronger voice was saying, 'He doesn't love you. He will never love you. He has chosen her instead of you. She is more beautiful than you are. If you keep living, you will see them happy and you will be miserable.'

To be honest, I don't remember if at the time I wanted to kill myself or just cut myself to numb the emotional pain I was feeling. I closed my eyes, thinking it wouldn't hurt as much if I wasn't looking. Just as the blade touched my skin, I heard an even stronger voice telling me to stop. I recognised it to be God's voice. Without hesitating I threw the pair of scissors across the room. I dropped to my knees and cried out to God, thanking Him for rescuing me.

You see, there are three ways the enemy sets out to harm you. He aims to steal, kill and destroy. One way he does this is by manipulating your thoughts. He will get into your head, if you let him, and persuade you to do things that are not of God. He knows the potential in you. He knows that God has called you to a purposeful and thriving life. He knows how much God loves you. He strikes the hardest in the stormy season, knowing this is when you are most vulnerable. This is the time when your feelings are overwhelming. This is when he tries to steal your faith. It's in these times that you need to draw close to God. Don't let the storms in your life decide your destiny. God has a plan for everyone, including you.

> 'For I know the plans I have for you,' declares the Lord, 'plans to prosper you and not to harm you, plans to give you hope and a future.'
> Jeremiah 29:11

This Bible verse says that the Lord has a plan and a purpose for your life. If you commit suicide, you will miss out on what God has planned for you. You will not be able to enjoy the wonderful purposes preordained for you. Nor will you be able to complete your unfinished business here on earth. God wants to prosper you in all areas of your life, and He wants to give you a great future. Who better to trust than your Creator? The One who knew you before you were born. The One who planned your life before you were even thought of by your parents. The One who created you as a unique human being.

So when dark thoughts come to mind,

> ...take captive every thought and make it obedient to Christ.
> 2 Corinthians 10:5

Ask Him to cast out any thought that does not come from Him. Those thoughts are like weeds. You need to pull them out before they start taking over. Ask Jesus to take them from you and throw them away. Only He has the power to do so.

I once heard it put like this: when you use a sieve, the

smaller particles sift through and the bigger ones stay behind. So it is with your mind – you can choose which thoughts you will allow in and which ones you will keep out. The smaller particles represent those thoughts that are positive and build you up, and the larger particles represent those that are destructive and tear you down. These larger particles include lies that have been told about you, things from your past that have hurt you, things you have done that you want to forget, and other troubling thoughts.

Ask yourself this important question: *Which thoughts am I allowing into my mind?* It might not be your current situation that is affecting you – it could be something from the past that is revisiting your thoughts. You need to forget what is behind you and press forward to what is ahead. You need to take those thoughts captive to Jesus Christ.

JUST BREATHE

At various times throughout my life I have had to deal with anxiety. I had my first panic attack when I was a child. It was so bad that I could not control it. It started with a tight chest, which led to wheezing and hyperventilating, and ended in a full-blown panic attack. It was really scary. I eventually learnt to control these attacks by using breathing exercises and other methods. By the time I reached my teenage years I thought all of that was behind me in. But then the anxiety reappeared, this time far more aggressively.

I remember the night I was at my boyfriend's home watching a movie, when suddenly I went completely limp and couldn't breathe. My hands went numb and tingly. My body started to shake with cold. But when I layered up, I instantly became hot again. I couldn't lift my arms above my head, I felt so weak. I was gasping for air. All I wanted to do was cry because of the fear, but crying only made the situation worse – so I had to force myself to remain calm and just breathe through it. I had never experienced these symptoms before.

My boyfriend's mother called the ambulance. The paramedics arrived and checked my blood pressure, breathing and sugar levels. They were all surprisingly normal. They told me that I was suffering from an anxiety attack and vertigo, and offered to take me to the hospital. But by this stage my symptoms had mostly subsided, so I decided to stay in bed and rest instead.

The next day we had been invited to a birthday party, and I was all dressed up and ready to go. But then, all of a sudden, my chest tightened and I couldn't breathe. Recognising what was happening, I broke down in tears, but this only made my breathing even harder to control. My boyfriend helped me with my breathing exercises, and this brought things back to normal again. By the time I had calmed down I felt weak and dizzy because of the lack of oxygen to my brain, and once again had to lie down.

I later went to the doctor, who made me complete a survey regarding my thought patterns. After he had calculated my score, he diagnosed a mild case of anxiety and prescribed some antidepressants. He also referred me to a psychologist. But the medication that I was prescribed was so strong that it made me feel like a zombie. I couldn't walk or function properly on it. I couldn't even get out of bed. And the panic attacks continued.

When I had a follow-up consultation with my doctor, he asked me to get a blood test done. The results showed that I had a fatty liver and that my iron level was low – so I was prescribed iron tablets. Also, my liver needed to be monitored every three to six months, and I was put on a diet and told to start exercising. By this stage I had started to feel really defeated. I felt like my body was always against me in some way. Because of my dietary restrictions, I could never enjoy eating or drinking what I enjoyed, like everyone else did. When dining out, I would have to ask the chef what ingredients were in the dishes.

Another serious panic attack occurred a few months later, and again I nearly ended up in hospital. That week my boyfriend had experienced a pretty serious seizure. After rushing over to his place in the middle of the night and seeing the aftermath of his episode, I became fearful, and nearly went straight into panic-attack mode. But I knew I needed to be strong for him, and that his family didn't need two people to look after that night, so I stopped it before it could properly start.

Two days later, the episode was still on my mind. So, in order to distract myself, I decided to go to a games evening with my Bible study group. On the way there I was feeling a bit breathless, but was determined to push through and enjoy myself. However, during the half-time break, I started to feel really bad. My face felt red and burning, but my friend told me it looked normal. I thought I needed a glass of water to keep myself cool, but when I tried to walk to the kitchen, I could barely stand. I took a seat, and went completely limp. I then started hyperventilating uncontrollably. One of the guys walked me over to a couch, where I lay back and tried to get my bearings, but everything was spinning rapidly. He told me that my pupils were dilated and my pulse was very weak. I kept getting hot flushes alternating with freezing sensations. It was weird.

Eventually they called an ambulance, and the paramedics performed a raft of tests. Everything came back normal, but I still wasn't feeling one hundred per cent. When they asked if I wanted to go to the hospital, I said 'yes'. As they walked me slowly down the stairs I started to feel nauseous as a result of the spinning sensation. This would be my first trip to the hospital in an ambulance as an adult.

I arrived at the emergency department and had to wait about thirty minutes before being seen. By this time my boyfriend, his mum, my mum, my best friend and my Bible study group leaders had all arrived to support me. They stayed with me until it was so late that they needed to leave in order to get some sleep before work the next day. I didn't get to see a doctor until about 5:30am, and by that time all my symptoms had vanished and I was feeling much better.

At this stage of my life I felt like I was trapped in a negative bubble that I couldn't get out of. I was so deep in that, no matter what people told me, I couldn't find any positives in my life. It felt like nothing was going well. At one point I even questioned my very existence, and asked myself, 'Is there *anything* good in my life'? I had lost my smile and my joy. This was a really tough time, and I had to learn to control my thoughts and think positively.

One person who made a huge difference to me was my psychologist. I trusted her, and although her sessions made me feel completely vulnerable on the one hand, they made me feel open and comfortable on the other. She helped me delve deeply into my issues and come up with solutions. She made me realise that everyone goes through anxiety, and that whilst I could not completely remove anxiety from my life, I could learn to control it by changing my way of thinking.

Hope in the Storms

One of the techniques I really found useful was called 'putting your thoughts on trial'. This is a very effective tool, one which I would recommend you use in your own lives. By using this technique, I learned to change my negative thoughts into positive ones, to see the bright side of what would otherwise have been a negative situation. It involves setting up an imaginary law court in your head, then grabbing a negative thought from your mind, and compiling a list each for the 'prosecutor' (who *supports* that negative thought, claiming it is *true*) and the 'defence' (who argues *against* that negative thought, saying it is *not true*). For example, one of my most common negative thoughts was, 'It's not fair. I'm living with this incurable disease and I can't eat what I want.' *This thought could be pretty strong in the moment that I felt it.* Below is a table with points from a prosecutor and a defence.

Prosecutor – 'for' that thought	**Defence** – 'against' that thought
There are so many foods I can't eat, due to their high sodium levels.	I have plenty of other sodium-low foods I can eat, like chocolate.
I am living with Meniere's disease, which is as yet incurable.	I can still drive to work and live a relatively normal life.
I am tired of living with illness.	I will have a healthy body one day.
Nobody can help me.	I believe God can supernaturally heal me.
I cannot eat what I want.	My symptoms have left or are less, and I am healthier on this diet.

I could list many more negative thoughts that I have changed using this technique, but I will leave you with just this one, so you can see how to do it.

In order to get myself out of my negative bubble, I tried to surround myself with positive people. Also, I learnt to affirm myself and not rely on other people's affirmations. I drew closer to God and read His word more often, thereby actively being in His presence. This brought me incredible peace and joy. I forced myself to start being motivated by refusing to lie in bed and feel sorry for myself. And slowly I started to find purpose in my life again. I began trying to focus on others. I found joy in the simple things. I tried to be grateful for every little thing in my life, and tried never to take anything for granted.

Every day I would wake up and say out loud something that I was grateful for; this was a great way to start each day. Yes, I still had 'off' days, but I learnt to control them by replacing the negative thoughts with positive and encouraging ones. I allowed in only those thoughts that built me up, and blocked those that tried to tear me down. Life was slowly looking good again.

LET'S SAY A PRAYER

Lord, I pray that you will protect my thoughts from the enemy. Take control of those thoughts that are not of you. Strengthen my faith, especially in the difficult times, when there seems to be no way out. Let me walk on your path, with you as my guide. Help me to understand that you have a great future for me, one that will prosper me. Help me to not fall into any temptation, or let anything enter my mind that is not of you. I give you full control of my thoughts and my mind. It is no longer I that live, but Christ who lives in me. Help me not to worry about tomorrow, because you are already there. Help me to live in the present and trust you each day. Help me to live each day with a thankful attitude. In Jesus' name I pray. Amen.

CHAPTER REVIEW

- Death is never the answer.
- Remember to put on the full armour of God (Ephesians 6:10–18), especially when you are feeling vulnerable.
- Remember who the real enemy is.
- God has a great purpose and future for your life.
- Everyone goes through anxiety and there are ways to control it.
- Only entertain positive thoughts; put your negative thoughts on trial.
- Have the right people supporting you.

Chapter 5
STANDING STRONG IN YOUR SINGLENESS

Trust in the Lord with all your heart and lean not on your own understanding; in all your ways submit to him, and he will make your paths straight.

Proverbs 3:5–6

And they all lived happily ever after... This is how every fairy tale ends. The two main characters marry, and everything is perfect. They never show the flaws or the disagreements in their story, and there is always a happy ending. Do not live in this fairy-tale reality. You will end up being disappointed. Yes, you can be happy with someone, but there will always be imperfections in the relationship because nobody is perfect.

I was in two relationships that I thought would actually amount to something serious. The reason the first one broke up was because it was a long-distance relationship. The second one didn't work out because there were differences over the ideal of having children; clearly we both wanted different things.

The first relationship was just too hard to keep going. It was a mutual break-up. I had been with this guy for about six months, and it was very hard to end it. About a month into this relationship he started complaining of sore eyes and headaches all the time. We consulted many different doctors, and in the end it turned out to be a brain tumour. So, instead of being all lovey-dovey with each other in the first few months, like most couples are, we found ourselves in and out of doctors' waiting rooms, hospitals and specialist appointments. It really wasn't fun, but it showed him that I was sticking with him through his trials, and that I wasn't going anywhere else.

As a result of this brain tumour, he missed his family and friends at home too much, and decided that he wanted to move back to be with them, with or without me. It was a very tough decision, but because we had only been together for about six months, and because my entire life was not able to be uprooted, we decided to end the relationship. I distinctly remember driving home just after breaking up and crying out to God, 'What is the matter, God? Don't you want me to be happy?' At this point I had really lost all hope, and didn't see any other possibilities for me out there. I saw myself being alone for the rest of my life.

Two years later, I dated five guys (at separate times, of course!), but none of the relationships worked out. I started blaming myself, saying, 'What's wrong with me?' I started losing hope in guys, thinking that there was no one out there for me. I felt hurt because my relationships never lasted long. I started to stereotype all guys, thinking they were all going to reject me. I didn't think I was pretty enough, and even considered enhancing parts of my body in order to make myself more attractive.

Every time God closed a door on a relationship it was hard, and it took me a while to get over it. But deep down I trusted He had someone better out there for me. And so it was – every time a relationship ended and a new one started, it was better than the previous one. Something that the previous guy lacked, the new one had.

Let me be totally honest with you. Being single was difficult, and I struggled with it quite a bit. However, I eventually got to a place where I valued my singleness and was happy being alone and independent. Initially, this was to a large part because I focused on my older sister, who at the time was struggling with *her* singleness more than I was. I hated seeing her so unhappy, and I tried my hardest to make her happy – buying her flowers on Valentine's Day, encouraging her in what she was doing, and keeping her hope alive that a great guy would come across her path. I stopped focusing on my own singleness. For a time, I was content with life.

However, as soon as my sister found her man and started dating him, my singleness became an issue once again. Now that she was happy and not a focus for me, I began to agonise over my own situation. I began falling into a deep hole. It seemed that everyone around me was in a happy relationship, whereas I was alone, with no guy to love me or show me affection. I found it really hard going to weddings and parties with no boyfriend. Although I wanted to celebrate with and be happy for my friends, it was very difficult to be truly pleased for them when I felt so left out.

When I went on Facebook and saw that someone I knew was now in a relationship, engaged, married or pregnant, I became jealous, despite trying to be supportive of them. I kept thinking, 'I want that. Why can't *I* have that?' Well-meaning friends told me, 'Your guy is out there somewhere,' or 'It will happen when you are least expecting it.' In return I used to think, 'It's *easy* for you to say that – you're married, or engaged, or in a relationship.' No one could give me the right advice or, if it *was* the right advice at the time, I just wasn't listening.

I started getting into online relationships, which was a huge step for me considering what had happened to me with that teacher. This involved talking to guys I'd never met before, then meeting them (alone, in a public place), and finally deciding if I wanted to continue the relationship in person. With each new relationship my walls went up higher, and I could never truly be myself. The issue of trust was still always a stumbling block.

When I was younger, I used to think it was bad to date guys randomly, and that I should wait until I found the one that God had chosen for me. This was the thinking in my church. I had read the book *I Kissed Dating Goodbye*, and had taken its message to heart. I used to think that Mr Right would just show up on my doorstep, or I would cross paths with him somewhere, and that would be it. It wasn't until I saw my counsellor and discussed my 'guy issues' that my eyes were opened.

She said that I was living in a fairy-tale world, and it wasn't reality. She told me my future husband wasn't going to knock on my door wearing a ribbon, like a present. She was the one who encouraged me to go out on dates, so I could grow from these experiences and learn exactly what I wanted in a partner. She also told me that the first guy that I dated wasn't necessarily going to be my future husband – and she was right. She helped me realise that there are many great, respectful and honourable guys out there. And that I wasn't going to find them by staying in my room every night.

I came to realise that it's okay to pray for specific qualities in a guy, and to create a list of attributes of one's 'perfect' man. You know you most likely won't get everything on that list, but at least you start to have a general idea of the qualities you are looking for. Besides, God knows what you need, even if it isn't on that list.

By the way, just in case you think that perfect man or woman exists, I'm sorry to tell you that they don't. We are all human; we are not perfect; we all make mistakes; we all have our faults and flaws. None of us is perfect. Marriage is about forgiveness and acceptance. It's about loving your partner unconditionally and not trying to change him or her. Remember that in the wedding vows it says 'for better or for worse'. There will be good days and there will be bad days, and it's all about supporting each other through thick and thin.

Two big dangers about being single again after a traumatic breakup are *going on the rebound* (starting a new relationship while still distressed by the ending of the last one; trying to forget that person by quickly engaging with another) or *settling* (taking up with anyone, suitable or not, rather than being left alone). Make sure you don't do either of these things. Both usually lead to unhappiness.

After a spate of unsatisfactory relationships, I made up my mind that I *had* to be married before I turned 30. I had just turned 26 at the time. So I found myself always looking around frantically for the right guy, becoming more and more desperate. I felt like there was a ticking clock in front of me, that I was getting older and running out of time. But then I snapped out of this negative and pressurised thinking, and came to understand that God *did* have someone for me.

I realised that even if I *were* over thirty and still not married, at least I would know I hadn't settled on someone that

God didn't have lined up for me. The wait would be so worth it. I would rather wait to be happily married to a great guy than be married young and with the wrong person. I found that the best way to deal with my singleness was to make the most of it and to enjoy my independence. So I decided to leave my church (after being there for 23 years) and to look for a new one – just to see who else was out there. And I found a great bunch of people who instantly made me feel part of the family.

In this new church family I met a great guy named Stan, and we went out on a few dates. I quickly realised he had unresolved feelings from a past relationship. Consequently my walls went up and I couldn't show my true self. As a result the relationship couldn't work and only lasted a few weeks.

This was the second relationship I had been in that felt like it could potentially work, and initially I saw a future with him. So it really hurt when all of a sudden it shut down. I was in shock for days after the break-up. It ended so quickly and took a long time to get over. I remember it like it happened yesterday.

At the time of dating Stan I was one of the leaders of a prayer group which was held at my house on Friday nights. At the same time a guy I had once known (with the same name – let's call him Stanley) came back into my life via a family member. After meeting up again we talked for a while and then I invited him to my prayer group. After that we would sometimes get together and jam on his guitar and work on the songs that I had written (many of which worked out to be better than we expected). We clicked really well. Whilst all this was happening with Stanley, I was still interested in Stan.

One night I perceived God was saying to me, 'What happens if *Stanley* is the right guy?' I shrugged this off because I thought Stan was that person. However, this word from God constantly played in my head. Also, I had been given a previous word from God in which He said, 'Stop looking to the left; stop looking to the right; I will bring him to you.' With Stan I had made the move myself by branching out and finding the church, whereas Stanley had came back into my life without my doing anything. Deciphering all of this was really hard.

Whilst all this was happening, the name Stanley kept leaping out at me. I saw the name on number plates, I heard it on the radio, and wherever I went I kept encountering people named Stanley – from the TV shows I watched (where the new character was Stanley) to the flowers I received at work from my sister (that were arranged by Stanley). This was getting freaky. I had two Stanleys that I really cared about in my life, and no idea which to choose. Then God closed the door on Stan. He knew that we weren't right for each other; I can see that clearly now. At the same time I felt such a strong connection with Stanley, greater than anything I'd ever felt with any other guy that I'd dated. I had so much more in common with him – he had all the qualities I had prayed for, and we were both on the same spiritual level.

Then one Sunday night just before a Hillsong service (when I was freaking out because I wanted to pursue a relationship with him and wasn't sure he felt the same way about me) I told him my feelings, and he reciprocated. This was great, and from then on we were officially in a relationship.

That night we started our journey together as boyfriend and girlfriend. It seemed to be everything I had prayed for. Everything that we faced we brought to the Word of God, which covered our relationship. We were both supportive of each other's future career plans and studies. We met each other's families, and it felt so right. His parents loved me as the daughter they had never had. I felt so welcomed and appreciated by them. My parents loved him too, and said that they thought we were a good match and that he was a nice, genuine guy. He was everything I had prayed for.

About two weeks into our relationship I had a really bad gastro virus that lasted longer than expected, which I talk more about in another chapter. Every single day of that illness Stanley was there for me. It was hard being so vulnerable because I am the type of girl who doesn't like to show weakness but prefers to remain strong at all times. But now I had no strength, and Stanley saw me at my lowest. I was as pale as a ghost at one point. I had no colour in my face. I had no make-up on. I could barely walk. Yet he still found me beautiful. Now that is a man! He drove me to my doctor's appointments. He picked me up from work when I couldn't drive. His support and help meant everything to me.

It all seemed to be going really well until one day I received a message from him saying he had concerns about our future as parents. He said that he couldn't see himself ever being a father and that he knew how important having children was to me. Growing up I could always see myself as one day being a mother, and I looked forward to it. So I knew that by staying with Stanley I would be 'settling'. We tried to compromise and work through it, but nothing worked. He said he would never want children, so I realised that I would have to either be okay with that or end the relationship.

It was a really hard decision, but I had to think about my future – and part of that was my desire to be a mother one day. So I ended it. After having that final chat with Stanley over the phone I remember coming downstairs to where my mum and sister were waiting to hear the result, and crying for hours with them. They both comforted and supported me through this breakup.

At this time it seemed that all of my friends were getting into relationships or getting engaged and married, and once again it was really tough for me to be supportive towards them. But I reached out and made the effort, despite my own sadness.

Do not 'settle' for any person just because you are getting older. Your future partner is out there somewhere. Don't give up praying and looking for him or her. Most importantly, don't lose your trust in God – He knows the best person for you. It might be someone you least expect. But God knows what He is doing. I knew that one day I would meet the right guy for me, and that he would want children, because that is a desire of mine. And I trust God to grant me the desires of my heart.

Stay strong in your singleness, knowing that the right person is waiting for you. They may not be the type of person you are normally attracted to, but God has a plan. Don't get distracted. Live in the moment, and you will find that your paths will cross in God's timing.

How did I handle my singleness? I re-joined my church, and started committing myself to God, and to the things I loved doing. I joined an awesome fellowship group, and surrounded myself with positive people. I started to focus on getting involved in things I enjoyed, rather than looking for guys. I built up my independence once again. I started doing things on my 'bucket list' – those things I'd always wanted to do. I took a trip to the snow for the first time. I joined an amateur theatre group (despite having no experience), and even managed to get a lead role, which is how I met my husband. I decided to write this book to encourage all you readers. *I found hope again in my singleness.*

LET'S SAY A PRAYER

Lord, I pray for my state of singleness. Sometimes it is really a struggle to watch my friends who are in relationships. Lord, I pray that I would see my singleness as a gift from you. I pray that I will remain strong in it, and use it as a time to draw closer to you. Let me also use it as a time to grow in my ministry and to worship you more. I pray for growth in my independence, and for many new opportunities. I pray that if I do enter into a new relationship and you then close the door on it, I will trust you and believe that you have someone better for me. I pray that I will not settle on just anyone. I believe that you have someone lined up for me, and I trust you to bring that person to me at the right time. Help me to worship you while I wait. I ask this in your name, Jesus. Amen.

CHAPTER REVIEW

- Use your singleness to be independent, and to cross things off your bucket list.
- Trust God when he closes doors on relationships. He knows what He is doing.
- DO NOT SETTLE.
- Everyone's timeline is different, so do not compare yourself to others.
- Keep praying for your future partner – God will bring that person into your life at the right time.
- Worship God while you are waiting.

Chapter 6
TWO YEARS TOO LONG

> We are hard pressed on every side, but not crushed; perplexed, but not in despair; persecuted, but not abandoned; struck down, but not destroyed.
> 2 Corinthians 4:8-9

Another enduring storm that I faced was an ankle injury which lasted for two long years. These felt like the most restricting and painful years of my life. I didn't fall over something, nor did I injure myself playing sport, nor even did I twist my ankle. It happened completely out of the blue, seemingly out of nowhere.

My boss and I had just come back from lunch, when all of a sudden I felt a sharp pain in my ankle. I thought it might just be a muscle spasm, so I tried to ignore it for the rest of the day. Having been through far worse pain than this, I thought at the time it was probably just a 24-hour thing that would resolve itself. But over the next few days the pain was not only still there, but was intensifying.

So I went off to the doctor to get it sorted out. But no matter which doctor, podiatrist or specialist I was referred to, none of them could diagnose the problem. They even took me to the hospital, where I was put in a private room so that about ten different doctors could examine me. I then had umpteen scans – yet none of these revealed anything. At the end of one full year, the scans were considered expired, and had to be redone.

It was absurd. Some doctors didn't even *believe* that I was in pain, because there was no medical evidence for it. I was labelled a 'mysterious case'. It was truly awful. I originally thought it would be over in a few weeks or months, but it lasted *two whole years*!

Many nights, especially in winter, I would cry myself to sleep – not only from the pain, but also from the frustration of not knowing where it came from. My parents hated seeing me in so much pain, and felt helpless because they couldn't do anything to ease it. My mum would constantly cry with me, because my pain would never leave, and she was at a loss to know how to help me. We would sit at our dining-room table, holding hands and just cry. She went with me to every scan and doctor's appointment, and she too felt the frustration of getting no diagnosis. I was so grateful that, whatever I was going through, my parents went through it with me.

The pain was non-stop, throbbing and intense. I was on crutches for most of those two years, because I could not put any pressure on my foot. I had new orthotics fitted to my ankle every few months, which needed to be re-adjusted at every fitting. It was all very repetitive, with no improvements. I had so many people praying over my ankle, but nothing was happening. I was not receiving the miracle that I so desperately needed.

I hated going everywhere on my crutches. I didn't mind going to work, where only my boss could see me; but when there were parties and other events happening, I preferred staying at home rather than being seen. I did go to a few Christian camps (where I couldn't get involved in any of the games or physical events), and to my best friend's 21st birthday party – because I was making a speech.

But in all those instances I felt like an idiot, and was very restricted. This wasn't my first time on crutches – I had injured myself many times before, which had often necessitated my needing them. So not only were people used to seeing me using them, but I was now a proficient crutch operator, able to do tricks such as walking backwards. I have so many funny and painful memories of being on them.

One of my bad memories of having the ankle injury at that stage of my life was that it spoilt my 21st birthday party. I had wanted to wear a formal dress and some nice high heels, but I was forced to wear flats. I was so upset that I bought a dress long enough to cover my feet, so that no one could see what shoes I was wearing. On the night itself I couldn't really move around much without being in pain. I was able to dance, but not for very long. However, despite this drawback, it still was a very memorable night for me.

At that time I was reading Nick Vujicic's book, *Life Without Limits*. I had seen this book in every bookshop, and I made a deal with myself that if I saw it one more time then I would buy it. The next time I was out shopping I saw it again, so I bought it; and my life has completely changed since reading it.

Despite being born without arms and legs, Nick has been used by God and gone to places that he would never have thought possible. He has touched so many people's lives. He has blessed so many with his story; he has touched so many hearts; he has dried so many tears and he has witnessed so many healings. I have always been inspired by this wonderful man of faith, and he is top of the list of people I want to meet before I die. What he has gone through, and how he overcame his handicap, is an incredible story.

He is a voice of hope and joy for so many people who have lost their will to go on. He has been such an inspiration to me. His story made me look at my life and say, 'What is your excuse?' I am so glad I read his book – it has changed me and hugely influenced who I am today. One of his most inspiring quotes is: 'If you cannot receive the miracle, then *be* the miracle.' I apply these words to myself in every storm that I face these days. I encourage all of you to read his book or watch his videos on YouTube. He will inspire you too.

Remembering this quote of Nick's when going through this long storm was so encouraging for me. I obviously was not receiving the miraculous healing of my ankle that I had been praying for, so instead I decided to soar above my circumstances and direct my focus on others. I would pray with people, encourage them and listen to them. Because I focused all my energy on other people, I was able to forget about my own pain most of the time. It brought joy back into my life to see answered prayers, and to see people in tears because of the encouragement I could speak over them. I would help other people with their problems during the day, and then come home and face my own problems at night – together with my Heavenly Father.

Over those two years I was able to have a few cortisone injections, which gave my ankle relief from pain for about two to three weeks each time. These injections were very painful. The needle would go deep into my ankle and then be rotated to the left and right. The other problem with them is that you are only supposed to have them administered up to three times in your lifetime, and no more. I had five of them! The first four were done in the doctor's surgery. The last one (I remember my dad being with me) was done using an ultrasound, in order to pinpoint the exact spot. When the needle went in, I felt something burst inside my ankle. It felt like a balloon slowly popping. I didn't know if it was a good feeling or not. I was worried because the previous four injections hadn't felt like that. However, from that day on I experienced no more pain. *I was finally free.*

Before this last attempt, I had really cried out to God and asked Him for healing. I had been at the end of my tether, feeling so defeated and destroyed, like I couldn't go on. I felt like giving up. I still find it amazing that no doctor has ever been able to diagnose my condition, even to this day. The pain came, stayed for two years, and then healing took place.

Just as the introductory verse for this chapter says,

> **We are hard pressed on every side,** *but not* **crushed; perplexed,** *but not* **in despair; persecuted,** *but not* **abandoned; struck down,** *but not* **destroyed.**
> 2 Corinthians 4:8–9

This is one of my favourite verses because it is so encouraging. It proves that you can be so far down in life but, with the Holy Spirit living inside you, you will never ever be completely destroyed or defeated.

If you remove each 'but not', it would then read: 'We are hard pressed on every side, perplexed, persecuted (and) struck down.' It doesn't sound like a very encouraging verse any more, does it? However, when you put the 'but nots' back in, this verse brings us hope again. Jesus brings us hope.

Hope in the Storms

Jesus *is* our hope. If you trust Him, He will never abandon you or let life destroy you. Yes, there will be storms in your life that will challenge you and push you to your limits, *but Jesus is your hope.*

LET'S SAY A PRAYER

Lord, I pray that you will help me to keep persevering through every storm I face. Even when the pain lasts longer than normal, I pray that you will help me to keep living one day at a time. Help me to focus my time and energy on other people, so that I can bring joy and hope to them. Help me be a miracle to others whilst I wait for my miracle to happen. Help me to never lose my hope in you. Help me to never feel defeated or destroyed. I pray for this in your powerful name, Jesus. Amen.

CHAPTER REVIEW

- Whatever you go through, your loved ones will go through it with you.
- Make the most out of your life, even in the presence of great pain.
- Remember the words of Nick Vujicic: 'If you cannot receive the miracle, then *be* the miracle.'
- Soar above your circumstances and focus your attention on others.
- You will *never* be completely destroyed or defeated if you have Jesus.
- Jesus is your hope.

Chapter 7
DOUBLE BLESSING

The Lord himself goes before you and will be with you; he will never leave you nor forsake you. Do not be afraid; do not be discouraged.
Deuteronomy 31:8

I thought long and hard before including this chapter in my book. It covers an embarrassing condition that I grew up with. I finally decided to go public with it when I realised that there were probably many other people who had gone through the very same difficult and painful storm and who, like me, were also too embarrassed to talk about it. And, most importantly, because with God's help I once again made it through successfully.

I was born with a small hole in the skin above my buttock area. I never told anyone about it because it didn't seem 'normal', and I was embarrassed by it. The only people who knew about it were my immediate family. Because I'd had it all my life, I was used to it, and would laugh and say that I was 'doubly blessed'. My parents would jokingly reply, 'If we sold you, we would be rich.'

It never caused me any pain until I was about 18 years old. I had just started a job as a receptionist, and spent long periods sitting behind a desk. This constant sitting started to cause me quite a bit of pain, to the point where eventually I could barely move. So once again I went off to see the doctor. He referred me to a specialist, who diagnosed the tiny hole as a pilonidal sinus. Apparently a small hair had fallen into the hole. This would normally be okay, but because the hair was so deep in, close to my spine, it was potentially very dangerous. If left untreated, it could lead to an infection near my spine, which could cause further complications.

Barely able to process this information, I was told I needed to have surgery on it the following week, seeing as it was an urgent case. This would be my first major operation, and it happened so quickly and unexpectedly that it felt surreal. Was this really happening to me, or was it a horrible dream? Sadly, it was real.

Those next five days went by so quickly. I find that when I am nervous about something, time seems to speed up. The day before the surgery, I walked into the hospital with my mum and my sister by my side, and got the admin papers signed. It still hadn't hit me that I would soon be there, having my first surgery. The severity of the situation was too much to fully take in. I wasn't prepared. I didn't want this. I wanted time to stop.

When I finally lay down in my bed that night, all I could think about was the next day. This was my first big surgery. I was scared of being 'gassed'. I was scared of waking up in pain and the anaesthetic wearing off. I was scared of being in a hospital alone. I couldn't sleep. All these thoughts were playing on my mind. Finally, I managed to catch a few hours of sleep.

The next morning I woke up, turned straight to my Bible

and started crying out to God in fear. The verse I read was so timely. It said:

> 'So do not fear, for I am with you; do not be dismayed, for I am your God. I will strengthen you and help you; I will uphold you with my righteous right hand.'
> Isaiah 41:10

As soon as I read it, I knew God would be by my side and that I would not be alone. No longer did I need to fear, because He was strengthening me and helping me. It was an incredibly strong and powerful verse, and the timing was perfect.

My parents and sister had taken the day off work to be with me; this meant the world to me. As I signed in, gowned up and lay in the bed ready to be wheeled into theatre, I realised that I *could* face this, and that God was with me. I felt as if I had been filled with incredible strength. As I said goodbye to my family and watched their faces vanish around the corner, I started to prepare myself.

I was wheeled into a room where I could see straight into the theatre. I sat half-up and looked inside – it was bright in there, and I could see a few doctors and nurses walking around in their robes, masks and surgical hats. It now suddenly all felt very real. They started prepping me for surgery; they put a cannula into my arm and briefed me about what would happen. The procedure would entail cutting a 15-centimetre hole into the already existing hole, removing the hair, and then packing the wound up with a dressing – to allow for healing to take place slowly, one centimetre at a time.

When they left me for a few minutes, I decided to pray. I closed my eyes and put my hands together on my chest.

The next second I felt two hands clasping mine – I distinctly felt all ten of the fingers. I opened my eyes. There was no one else in the room except me. *I knew they were God's hands.* He was with me, just like He had promised. This made me feel even more secure. The nurse then came back and put the anaesthetic into my cannula. Counting down, I quickly drifted off.

When I woke up, I burst into tears of relief. The surgery was over, and I had made it, thankfully with no pain. My family came in one at a time to see me. It was the best thing in the world to see their faces again. I was then wheeled into my own private room, where I stayed overnight.

DON'T PANIC

The next morning the nurses wanted me to have a shower while they changed my sheets. I waited for Mum to arrive so that she could help me. As soon as I turned the shower on and the hot water hit my back, my whole body instantly became numb, and I started to lose my vision. My heartbeat started speeding up rapidly, getting louder and louder. Everything else around me became silent, until all I could hear was my heart pulsing.

I started wheezing, and felt that I couldn't breathe. I was starting to have a panic attack. Everything started spinning. I turned to my mum, barely able to get the words out, 'Mum, get the nurse.' She immediately pressed the emergency button, and after that I vaguely remember seeing some blurry figures bursting into the room. I felt someone wrapping me in a towel, and remember being placed on my bed and having a breathing mask strapped on to me. The last thing I saw before I passed out was Mum being ushered out with a most worried look on her face. I wanted to run and hug her, and tell her that everything would be fine. But I couldn't move. I could feel the tears streaming down my face as I slowly drifted away. I don't remember anything after that.

When I woke up, my bed was in a weird position – the bedhead was nearly touching the floor. They were trying to drain the blood back to my brain. I still had the mask on my face, but by this stage I was breathing normally again. Everyone looked calmer now, though I could see that my sister had a red face from crying. The first thing I did was to ask for ice because my throat was so dry from having had the breathing mask on.

Mum told me that she had been afraid because the nurses had been busy bringing the defibrillator machine in, in order to shock me into waking up. I'm so glad that did not happen. I thank the Lord for waking me up before then. As much as I wanted to go back home that day, they decided to keep me there another night in order to monitor my condition.

DRESSED FOR THE OCCASION

After all that excitement was over, the nurse came in and told me that she was going to replace my dressing. I had no idea what to expect. Mum stayed because she knew how nervous I was, and I'm so glad she did. Taking the old dressing off was painless, but putting the new one in was excruciating – it felt as if thirty needles were being jabbed into that area. All I could do was cry, and push through the pain. When the nurse told me that the dressings needed to be changed *every day for about two weeks*, I dreaded the thought of it. Going through all that pain everyday would be a nightmare – but I had no choice but to endure it, as that was the only way to reach full recovery.

Well, *six* weeks went by, and I was *still* having the dressings replaced. For the first few days it was done at the hospital, but after that a nursing service replaced the dressing at my home. One of the nurses was too rough, so I rang up the company and told them never to send her again. After about three weeks the new nurse decided it was time to show Mum how to do it. Though initially nervous, she picked it up really quickly, and was really confident by the end of it.

I took six weeks off work; thankfully my boss understood. I couldn't stand up properly, nor could I sit down comfortably. It was a really awkward situation. When people asked what the problem was, I was quite embarrassed, and just told them that I had had surgery on my lower back. I found out later that it is a fairly common condition amongst people of European ancestry, although more usual with men rather than women. I've often found myself in one of these 'less likely' categories. I've repeatedly heard doctors say, 'I've never seen this before,' or 'I've never seen this located in that area before.' Either way, my medical history has many times revealed something unusual or unique about me!

Within a few months my scar was healing perfectly, and there remained only a residual amount of pain. Even today, if I sit down on a hard surface, it can still be quite painful. But at least everything has healed. I like having scars on my body – they show that I have been through tough times and that they did not destroy me, but only served to make me stronger.

As you already know, I have suffered from panic attacks many times. I remember the first one like it happened yesterday. It was a Friday night, and I was at youth group with my sister. We were running around playing games. I remember turning to my sister privately and saying, 'I can't breathe.' Not knowing what to do, she took me outside to get some fresh air. Each step I took just made my situation worse. As soon as I stepped outside, I could feel something building up inside me. My chest was so tight that I felt like I was suffocating. I started to wheeze uncontrollably, and collapsed on the stairs, my hands covering my face. My sister screamed for help.

Luckily for me the youth leader at the time was a nurse, and knew what to do. Very calmly, she told me to follow her breathing pattern, using her hand as a guide for me to follow. When I was supposed to breathe in, she lifted her hand up, and when I was supposed to breathe out, she lowered it. She kept telling me that everything was going to be okay, and she was most reassuring. All the while, I kept one eye on my sister, who in turn was being comforted by our friends. I wanted to get up and hug her, but all I could manage at that point was myself. Within five minutes I was back to normal. It was a very scary experience. Even though it only lasted a short time, it felt much longer.

The next panic attack took place when I was in the Philippines on a mission trip. It was a really hot day, and I felt like I was suffocating again. Luckily there was a doctor in my team, and he sat me down and helped me to start breathing normally again. Sometimes these panic attacks happened when my sister was there to help – she had trained herself from past experiences. Other times Mum took control of the situation. When I was alone, I would use a paper bag; I could hear and monitor my breathing patterns using it.

I still occasionally experience panic attacks, but now I know how to control them. As soon as I feel one coming on,

I take slow, deep breaths and reassure myself that I am not going to die – this is so important because at the time you feel like you are suffocating. I then sit myself down and lower my head, so that the blood returns to it. When I feel like I am okay again, I get up very slowly, so I don't feel dizzy or faint.

If you suffer from this same debilitating condition, you probably have your own method of dealing with it. As long as it works for you, keep doing just that.

Just remember that no matter what you go through, God is always there. You might not physically feel His presence like I did, but all you have to do is believe He is there, and He will you give you a sense of reassurance and peace.

LET'S SAY A PRAYER

Lord, I pray for this surgery coming up. I know that you are with me and that I do not have to fear. I pray that you will guide the surgeon's hands, and let the procedure be a successful one. I pray for a quick recovery, and that you will help strengthen me through any pain that I might experience. I pray for strength during and after the surgery. I pray that I will learn to love my scar (if I have one) – because it will remind me that I need never feel defeated. Be with me Jesus, I pray. Amen.

CHAPTER REVIEW

- God is always with you, so do not be afraid.
- Pain is never a pleasant thing, but it won't last forever.
- Develop a spirit of perseverance to push through the pain.
- You will get better at controlling your reactions to your storms.
- You are in control of your anxiety.

Chapter 8
TAKEN TOO SOON

The LORD is close to the broken-hearted and saves those who are crushed in spirit.
Psalm 34:18

At some point in their lives, everyone loses someone or something dear to them. There are many different categories of loss:

- death of a family member or friend
- living with chronic illness
- death of pets
- mental or emotional breakdown
- loss of home or belongings
- job loss
- physical handicap, such as losing sight or hearing.

I went through a prolonged season of loss when my 80-year-old Nonna Clara passed away. Nonna Clara was my dad's mum. She lived with us for a long time whilst my siblings and I grew up. This was probably one of the most traumatic emotional storms I have had to face so far in my life. I remember one day getting a phone call from her; she had just had a comprehensive medical examination, and the doctor had given her a clean bill of health. I was so thankful to God for this, and was praising Him and rejoicing over this good news. But one week later the wind changed direction, and a hurricane was headed our way.

On that inauspicious day my parents sat my brother, sister and me down at our kitchen table, and told us the devastating news that the doctors had found cancer in Nonna's brain, and that she had only about six months to live. I remember it like it happened yesterday. The cancer was apparently spreading in her brain, and there was nothing they could do to stop it. She had just been given a clean bill of health, and now she was dying. We all went from a 'high' to such a huge 'low' within a few seconds. It was a huge shock to our entire family. To make matters even worse, about half an hour before hearing this awful news, someone very close to me had told me something really shocking – so now I was confronting *two* very serious situations at the same time. I was in double shock. My body felt numb.

Nonna's body was very fragile, and the radiation she was undergoing wasn't helping her. She started to feel really sick; the side-effects were too strong for her body to handle. She eventually told the doctors she didn't want any more radiation therapy. She was then moved into a nursing home because she couldn't look after herself anymore.

I remember helping with cleaning out her house and removing all the furniture, until nothing was left. It was so silent. We had made so many happy memories together there – our many sleepovers, cooking gnocchi together, playing games like rummy, and listening to her many stories of growing up in Italy. Seeing the emptiness of her house, I felt them come rushing back, and the immensity of it all become overwhelming. I scanned the empty room in slow motion, taking in every precious memory. I was the last one to leave. I closed the door behind me, and it was over.

Whilst in the nursing home, she kept saying, 'I want to go home.' But there was no home left for her to go back to. This nursing home was now her new temporary home. It was so hard watching Nonna slowly deteriorate in front of our eyes. With each new day she was forgetting more and more. She started losing hair, refusing to eat, and slowly losing her personality – to the extent that she just wasn't the same person any longer. She was in palliative care by this stage. The Nonna I had known and loved didn't exist anymore. That same Nonna with whom I had enjoyed having sleepovers, playing cards, picking fruit and shopping with was no longer there. Where was she? Where had she gone? Why did cancer have to take over her brain? These questions saddened me deeply.

Then one day at work I received a phone call from my dad telling me to come to the nursing home urgently because these could be the last few hours we would have with her before she passed away. I picked up my sister from college and rushed to the nursing home, all the while thinking, 'What if she dies before I get to say goodbye?'

As I entered the room, I saw my parents and brother crying. I looked over at the nearly lifeless body on the bed, and didn't recognise her. Nonna was by now completely bald, her gaze was frozen and she looked like a skeleton. That awful image will never leave me. The only way we could tell she was alive was because her chest was moving up and down; other than that she seemed lifeless. Although this was so frightening to see, I couldn't look away. I was in deep shock and disbelief that this was the Nonna I had grown up knowing and loving, and with whom I had shared so many treasured memories.

My parents gave each of us a chance to talk to her. When my turn came, I couldn't speak; I didn't know what to say. I just sat there holding her hand. At that moment I just wanted to wake up from the nightmare. I pinched myself, and knew I wasn't dreaming; this was reality. I didn't know if she could hear me, but I started to talk to her. As I talked, I looked into her eyes, which were glazed over. It was like staring into a dark hole – empty and endless.

My family and I stayed with Nonna for a few hours, mostly not speaking, just sitting in silence. Then came the time to say our final goodbyes. Tears were streaming uncontrollably down my face. My heart felt like it was going to jump out of my chest. I didn't want to say goodbye. I wanted to lie down next to her and stay there forever. I wanted to be hugged by her one last time. But that wasn't possible. I don't remember what I said to her, but I know that she was listening. I didn't know how I could walk away from her, but somehow I did. I took one last look back at my Nonna's lifeless body, and that was it. The next few days were a countdown. We didn't know how much time she had left, but it wasn't long. Three days later she passed away. Her suffering was finally over.

We didn't have a funeral for her because she hadn't wanted one; we respected her wishes. We sprinkled her ashes in our garden, the place she had loved so much – where she had spent so much of her time tending to the flowers and talking to the animals.

MOVING ON

The first few days and weeks were the hardest. The headaches I had from crying seemed endless. I missed her so much; I just wanted her back. I felt numb, like part of me was gone. I just couldn't move on. Time seemed frozen.

There are many different ways of coping with loss. Everyone grieves in his or her own way. In our case, each family member grieved in a different way – some of us kept our minds busy, others wanted to be around other family members, and yet others pushed everyone away and isolated themselves. I fitted into the last category; no one could have done or said anything to make me feel better at that time; I needed to be alone.

Being a Christian, I had my church family supporting me through this. They were praying for us, which we all greatly appreciated. But at the time, when it was all still so fresh, I found it hard to listen to Bible verses, or to well-meant clichés such as 'Everything happens for a reason' or 'She's in a better place now'. As a chaplain, I have learnt that people don't want to hear these things when they are dealing with grief. They rather want their feelings to be validated and normalised. One of the worst things someone can say to a person who is grieving is, 'I know what you are going through.' They cannot know, because every experience is different, and each person's reaction to that situation is different. No one will understand exactly what another is going through – except for our Father in heaven.

The first time back at church after losing my Nonna was the hardest. Everyone kept coming up to my family and me, hugging us and giving us their deepest condolences. Then someone unexpectedly grabbed me and hugged me for about five minutes without letting go. Normally a hug lasting that long would make me feel uncomfortable and awkward, but this hug had so much emotion and empathy in it that it brought healing to my empty places. It was a beautiful thing, one I will never forget. It was the *only* thing which really helped my grieving, and it was the *last* thing I ever expected would help.

There is only one 'person' who knows exactly what you are going through, and that is God. He feels your heartache. He understands exactly what you are going through. He walks every step with you, whether you are dragging your feet and barely making it, or walking by faith, one step at a time. He is right there, going through the entire grieving process with you.

One night I was in my room crying uncontrollably. Then all of a sudden it just stopped. It was as if everything went into slow motion – I saw my last tear hit the ground, and felt God wanted me to witness its falling. I then remember grabbing a pen and paper and writing down how I was feeling at the time, turning it into a poem/song which I called 'God's Lullaby'. It felt as if God was holding me in His arms like a baby, and singing me to sleep. I saw an image of Him rocking me. I felt such an amazing peace. And I *knew* that I was going to get through this time of grief safely.

Here is the poem that I wrote:

When all my tears have hit the ground
There's no more tears to cry
That's when He holds me in His arms
And sings me a lullaby
When all my faith is shaken

And my heart is unsure
He calms my own anxious heart
And gives me strength to endure
God's lullaby
What a beautiful song
The strings of His heart play a melody of love
That reaches to my soul
He cradles me
He sings me to sleep
When all my storms surround me
And the seas begin to rise
That's when He lifts me up on eagle's wings
And teaches me to fly

Maybe you who are reading this have recently experienced the loss of someone or something you loved dearly. Unfortunately, loss is a normal experience in all of our lives. I am so sorry that you are going through this, and I cannot imagine what you are experiencing right now. At this overwhelming time, things may seem like they will never get back to normal, and you may feel like you just want to give up. You may see everyone else moving on in life, and feel like you are stuck.

As a chaplain, I have learnt that there is no timeline for grieving. You must allow yourself to grieve for as long as it takes. Everyone deals with grief differently, and no two people behave the same way. When you come to a time when you are able to start making changes in your life, that is when you will know that you are coping with your grief, albeit one slow day at a time – and that is a great step in the right direction, towards healing and recovery.

Five years after my Nonna Clara's passing, I had another

encounter with grief, this time with the death of my grandfather (whom we called Poppy). He was from my mum's side. Poppy and I shared a common problem – we both had to face many illnesses in our lives; in this he reminded me of myself quite a bit. Growing up, I remember him spending much of his time in hospital with illnesses the doctors found difficult to diagnose.

One morning I was at work catching up on last-minute emails before driving out to Sydney airport for a work trip to Brisbane. I hadn't been looking at my phone, but suddenly noticed that I had missed two calls from Mum. She usually worked on the night shift, so she should have been asleep at that time. I rang her back, my heart pounding with anxiety at the timing of her calls. She didn't sound her normal cheerful self, and I could hear that she had been crying. 'Poppy passed away last night in his sleep,' she told me. Immediately I dropped to the floor, the phone still in my hand, and we cried together. I was in shock and disbelief. One minute he had been here, and the next minute he was gone.

The Brisbane trip was cancelled, and instead my parents picked me up from work and we went to the hospital where his body was. Nanna J (Poppy's wife) and my aunt were also in the car. We drove in silence most of the way there; nobody felt like talking; everyone felt numb. On arrival we found his body lying on the bed, his face discoloured. This was the first time I had seen a dead body, and it was frightening for me. My Nanna J took one look at him, went over and gave him a kiss on the forehead, and left the room. I went with her to comfort and support her; everyone else stayed in the room with Poppy.

By this stage I had learnt a great deal in my chaplaincy

course about grief and loss, so I utilised these skills to help Nanna J get through her grief. I spoke to her about Poppy, thereby keeping happy memories of him fresh and alive. I asked her questions about their life together. I consoled her. I cried with her. But mostly we just sat in silence together, which was peaceful and healing for us both.

The next few days, weeks and months were difficult for both my Nanna J and my entire family. I didn't really give myself the space to grieve, because I was helping everyone else with their grieving. I was the 'rock' that everyone turned to for hugs, empathy and 'venting' sessions. Even to this day, Nanna J still thanks me for everything I did for her that day at the hospital and every day after that. I am so glad I could have been there for her when she needed it the most.

When you go through a season of grief, remember that each day that goes by does get a little easier. I am not saying that there won't be setbacks; there *will* be things that trigger memories of your loved one – birthdays, anniversaries, familiar smells, and many other things. But you will find that when you revisit those memories they won't affect you to the same extent that they did when the grief was very fresh; they won't cripple your ability to survive.

The anniversaries of Nonna Clara's and Poppy's birthdays still trigger memories and feelings for me. The first year was probably the hardest. But, a few years on, I'm a lot stronger, and the memories are less painful. In the first few years after their deaths, I couldn't watch old videos of myself with Nonna Clara or Poppy, or look at photos of them without crying uncontrollably, whereas now there are fewer tears.

I promise you that it does get better. Sadly, nothing can bring the person or people back, but good memories allow you to hold on to them and reflect on the good times you had together. Something else I have learnt about grieving is that we shouldn't allow anyone else to prescribe how or how long we grieve. Remember, *everyone grieves differently*. Find a way to deal with your loss. For me, it was writing songs or journaling. Once again, everyone is different. Find something that works for you.

LET'S SAY A PRAYER

Lord, this is a really hard storm to face. I cannot believe that I have lost _____. I pray that, as I am grieving, you will be close by my side. I pray for your comfort during this time. I pray that, as each day passes, the pain will slowly decrease. I pray that each day you will help me take one step forward. I pray that your love and joy will restore every part of me that is broken or missing. I pray that you will help and encourage me during this period of grief. It says in the Bible that if I draw close to you, you will draw close to me (James 4:8). Lord, I need you. Help me at this time. I pray this in Jesus' name. Amen.

CHAPTER REVIEW

- Everyone deals with loss in their own way.
- There is no schedule for grieving.
- Nobody except God will ever understand exactly what you are going through.
- He will bring comfort to your grieving heart.
- Take it one step at a time.

Chapter 9
THERE IS ALWAYS A RAINBOW AFTER THE STORM

> He has made everything beautiful in its time.
> Ecclesiastes 3:11

I remember how after losing Nonna I couldn't walk into a hospital or nursing home again for a long time. The smells and sounds were too familiar; they brought back terrible memories of my family visiting her when she was lying in bed nearly lifeless. It was a very scarring image, one that would never leave me.

A year after her death I enrolled in a Christian college to do a chaplaincy course, and was very excited about it. A brand new year, with all of its new opportunities and adventures lay before me. I was really looking forward to moving on to a new phase in my life.

I started my first day without knowing anyone, out of my comfort zone, but thankfully made new friends quickly. It's amazing what happens when you get together with people who have similar goals and passions as you, who share a desire to serve others. The course I had signed up for involved finding placements in institutions in the community where we could volunteer for work experience. We had to find these placements ourselves. One lecturer suggested that a good place to work would be at a hospital. I cringed. That was the last place I wanted to be, and I just didn't think I could cope with it.

I tried calling different schools, with no luck. I then tried various universities and colleges, but still had no luck. I even spoke to someone in the Salvation Army, but that too proved fruitless. I tried everywhere I could think of in order to avoid approaching a hospital. The deadline was getting closer, and I still hadn't been booked in anywhere. So, very hesitantly, I finally rang a hospital, and they agreed to allow me to volunteer for the required number of hours needed for my course, spread over six months. As soon as I had been booked in, I looked up to God and said, 'Really? Why now? I really don't want to do this, but seeing this is the door you have opened for me, I will trust you.'

The following week, on my first day of volunteering at the hospital, I remember driving there and praying as I went – asking God to help me get through that day and the next six months. I was so afraid to step back into a hospital environment, but I knew it had to be done. I had always known I would eventually have to face this fear, and now God had chosen this time to help me accomplish it.

Suddenly there I was, standing outside the electronic doors at the entrance to the hospital. I took a deep breath and walked in. All the familiar sights, sounds and smells greeted me – the beeping of machines, the cool air-conditioned rooms, the sounds of equipment being wheeled around, the smell of hospital food and the sight of blood and needles. It was all so real and so confronting.

The role of student hospital chaplain was initially quite a confronting one for me. I started off by visiting patients that

I had never met before. I didn't know what condition they were in or how long they had been in hospital. Some of them didn't want to talk because they were in pain, others yelled at me to get out of their rooms, and yet others kept their curtains drawn because they wanted to be left alone. I had to face quite a bit of rejection early on.

However, there were many amazing opportunities that God gave me. I was able to talk to patients, listen to their stories, care for them and even pray for some of them, which was incredible. I loved visiting the women's wards because most of the patients there were very open and happy to talk. But my favourite place was the emergency department. People there were frustrated – many had been waiting for long periods (sometimes hours) just to be seen, so I became their 'venting machine'. They would share their frustrations with me and I would try to help them in any way possible, whether it be getting them a drink, blanket or food (if they were allowed to eat), checking their waiting time, finding out information for them or just simply listening. I loved being available to help them out.

I faced a confronting situation one day whilst helping a couple. The husband was suffering from dementia, and kept asking me the same question over and over again. Out of the corner of my eye I noticed his wife, in tears because she couldn't handle it anymore, hiding behind her newspaper. I was able to comfort her whilst still talking to her husband.

At one point he reminded me of Nonna, with her similarly lifeless eyes, lying on her deathbed. It was very confronting; her death was still very recent. It was too much for me to handle at that point, so when it was appropriate I found an excuse to leave. I immediately sought out the head chaplain and I told her how this interaction had affected me. She was really supportive in helping me work through my feelings, and even gave me the rest of the day off.

Apart from that one particularly confronting situation, I loved my role as a student hospital chaplain. I look back now and thank God for providing me with that time there. It was a rainbow of hope after my stormy season of loss. If I hadn't confronted my fear of hospitals, I never would have been able to meet all those amazing people and pray with them. It definitely was a memorable experience, one that I readily share with others.

As the title of this book suggests, God can be *your* hope during the storm. And, as the title of this chapter suggests, He will bring you a rainbow at the end of it, just like He did for me, if you simply ask Him. Every day on my way to the hospital I would pray that God would make me hopeful and expectant, and that He would open doors and provide opportunities for me to grow. And He always answered those prayers. He is so good.

Another fear I faced at that time was going back into a high school. I wasn't bullied at school, but neither did I have the easiest experience. I wasn't part of the 'cool' group, and much of the time I felt overlooked. I was just 'there', if that makes any sense to you. I was just a name on the roll, a face in the classroom, and a photo in the yearbook. I knew God wanted me to confront those feelings of having been overlooked and invisible by volunteering as a student chaplain at a high school.

I contacted somebody I knew, who then connected me with a particular school. I had heard bad things about it and about the area it was located in, so understandably was fearful when they accepted me as a volunteer chaplain. But, once again, I said a prayer, took a deep breath, and entered the school gates determined to face my fears. I stepped out in faith.

I'm glad I did, because God provided me with amazing opportunities to gain rapport with the students, to the point that they trusted me and opened up about personal things. Some of them even allowed me to pray with them and befriend them. I had the special responsibility of overseeing the games at their breakfast club once a week, and this afforded me the opportunity to bond really well with the students in the younger years. I made those mornings great fun for them, and I loved spending that time with them – so much so that I continued volunteering my services there the next year, long after my placement was over.

Walking back into high school again, this time not as a student but as a trainee chaplain, was an amazing experience. This time around I didn't feel like I was being judged. I knew that God had placed me there for many reasons, not the least being to confront my unresolved issues from the past, but also to listen to and care for those students who needed it. What an incredible honour it was.

Maybe there is something that you are holding on to, that you are not yet ready to face. That is alright, but try to think of the opportunities that you might be missing out on because of that fear. It may be fear around starting a new job, or starting college, or getting married, or having a baby, or something quite different. Don't hide behind your fear; don't allow it to rule your life. Step out in faith, knowing that God will be with you, and will open up doors of opportunity and growth for you ... because He *will*.

NEAR DEATH EXPERIENCE

I remember an incident when Mum, my sister and I were returning from visiting our friend in hospital. The weather on the way home was crazy. It was raining heavily. There must have been oil or grease on the road surface, and this resulted in our car skidding uncontrollably, and we ended up spinning a few times before coming to an abrupt halt. It all seemed to happen in slow motion. I was sharply aware of every second of this near-death experience. When we came to our senses, we found we had landed on a traffic island, in between a pole and a tree. Amazingly, we were completely unscathed – not a scratch on either the car or our bodies. The only damage was to the hubcap, which had come loose and rolled down the street. Other than that, we were totally unharmed.

I remember my mum being really shaken. She first checked we were okay; then she got out and checked to see if there was any damage to the car. She was too traumatised to retrieve the car, so she knocked on a nearby door and a nice gentleman drove it back onto the road for us.

God was definitely watching over us that night – the situation could have been quite different if He hadn't been. It was crazy to think that if another car had been on the street at the same time, or if we had ended up one metre further to the left or right, the outcome would have been disastrous. It was a very scary experience, and at the time it was happening we thought the worst. But praise God for keeping us safe.

My parents once told me about their near involvement in a tragic incident – one of the worst railway accidents in Australian history. The day it took place is now remembered as 'The Day of the Roses'. A train coming from the Blue Mountains was headed towards Sydney. As it passed through the town of Granville, it derailed and rammed into the supports of a bridge, causing it to collapse on two of the carriages. This resulted in the tragic deaths of 83 people and the injuring of over 200 others.

Mum and Dad were very nearly involved in that accident. Mum was *supposed* to be on that train, but was late and missed it, and Dad *was* on that train but got off a few stops before Granville. It's crazy to think if my mum had caught that train and if my dad had stayed on for a few more stops, they might not be here today. And neither would I! The next time you are stopped by the traffic lights or are too late to catch a train, be thankful. You just don't know – it might be that God has intervened to save your life!

YOU ARE THE VOICE

Some time back I met a guy at a church outreach. He told me that he had been a drug addict, and as a consequence had nearly died in an accident after racing his high-performance car. This resulted in him being so badly injured that he had since been confined to a wheelchair. He hated being stuck in it, and just wanted his life to end. He told me that he had nearly died three times during the accident, but that he believed God would not let him go. He kept asking me, 'Why didn't He just let me die?'

There must be a reason for this. Perhaps he could be a voice for teenagers or young adults who have similar addictions or who love to race dangerously in their cars. I just don't know, but God does.

His story reminds me of another guy, one whom I have already told you about in an earlier chapter. His name is Nick Vujicic. Nick was born without arms and legs. In his book *Life*

Without Limits he talks about the struggle that he had growing up feeling different. He tells how he tried to kill himself one night by drowning himself in the bathtub. But God didn't want his life to end; He wanted Nick to fulfil his purpose on earth and to be a testimony of His love and healing to others. And that is what Nick is doing today. He is travelling all over the world visiting different countries and cultures, preaching the gospel of Jesus Christ to them. He is bringing life and hope back into people's lives, and spreading joy wherever he goes. He is being a role model to others.

No matter what you have gone through in life, God can heal you and use you to help others. You have a unique purpose here on earth. Whatever storm you go through, there will always be a rainbow at the end of it, if you let God help you.

LET'S SAY A PRAYER

Lord, I pray that when fear causes me to turn my back on new opportunities, you will replace that fear with your perfect love. It says in the Bible (1 John 4:18) that your perfect love drives out all fear. Help me not to hide behind my fear. Help me to step out of my comfort zone. Help me to have the courage to take that leap of faith, knowing that you will catch me, and that you will open new opportunities for me. I pray that I will be able to face my fears knowing that you are my strength, my comfort and my joy. I pray that, whatever storm I face, there will be a rainbow at its end. I pray this in the name of Jesus. Amen.

CHAPTER REVIEW

- Step out of your comfort zone in order to experience new growth.
- Confront your fears head-on.
- Remember that there is always a rainbow after the storm.
- Sometimes God allows setbacks for a reason.

MRI revealing my 'potato-looking' tumour
(egg shape, bottom left) sitting on the nerve.

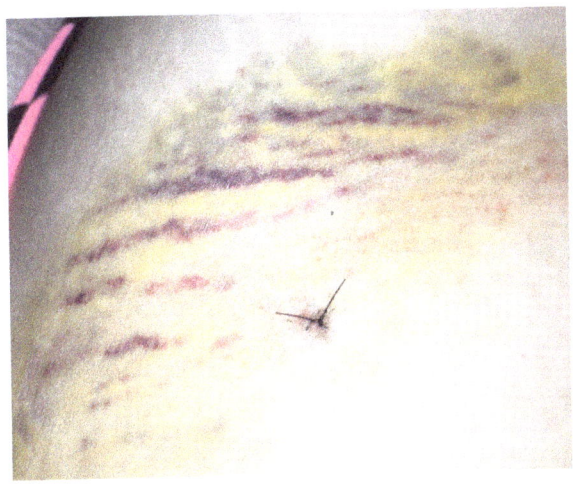

X marks the spot for the biopsy.

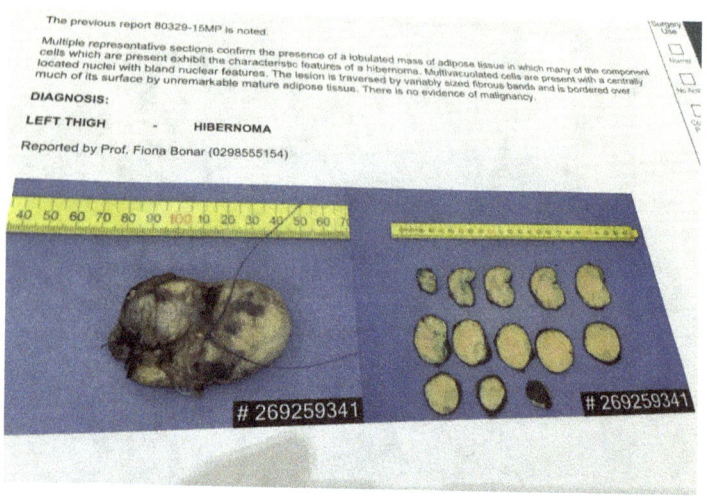

The hospital report showing my benign hibernoma tumour (left) and the tumour chopped up (right) after it was removed.

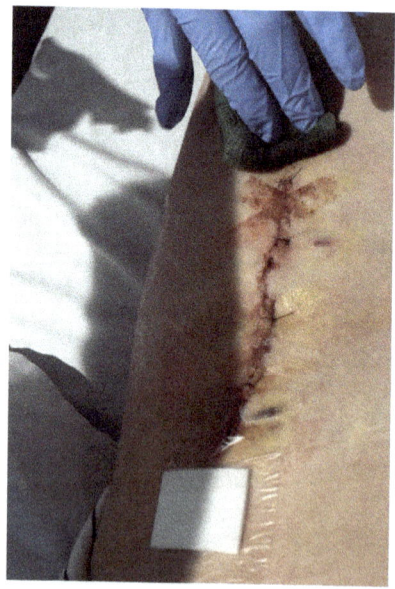

Stitches after tumour removal.

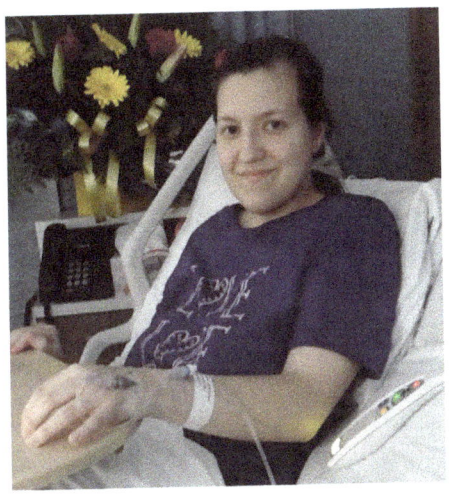

*Day two of being in hospital after tumour removal.
No pain.*

*With Gerry Roberts, who inspired me and taught me
the essentials for writing a book.*

Hope in the Storms

This is my mum. She has been with me through every storm I encountered.

This is my dad. He has taught me how to be strong in my faith through every storm.

Photos

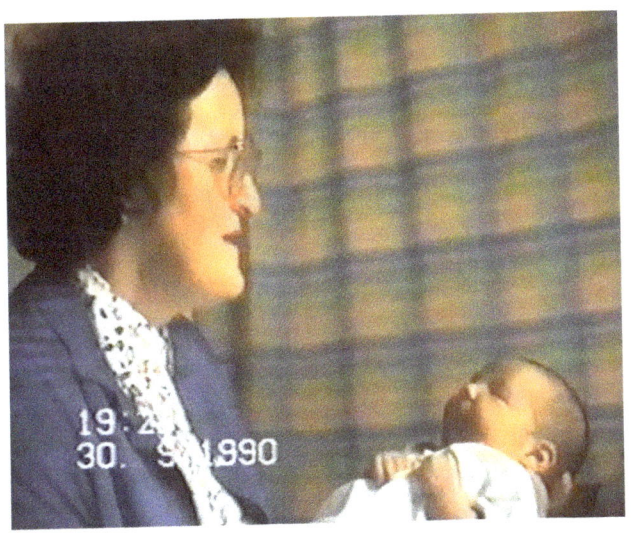

My Nonna Clara, whom I lost to cancer. I miss her so much. This was the first moment she held me after I was born.

My big sister, Lee Lee. She has spoken many words of guidance over my life.

Sharing a speech at my friend Ella's 21st birthday with crutches. Nothing stops me.

My amazing friends, Adrian and Annalie, who are also leaders with me in a prayer group.

Photos

My big sister, Melissa. She has always been there to encourage me and support me.

My best friend, Lenie. We have always kept God at the centre of our friendship.

*My amazing husband, Dan, whom God has brought into my life.
He always keeps me smiling, positive and hopeful.*

*This is one of my favourite photos.
This is what true worship is. I was so lost in His presence,
that it didn't matter what storm was surrounding me.*

Chapter 10
BIRTHDAY SURPRISE

> Not only so, but we also glory in our sufferings, because we know that suffering produces perseverance; perseverance, character; and character, hope. And hope does not put us to shame, because God's love has been poured out into our hearts through the Holy Spirit, who has been given to us.
> Romans 5:3-5

For a few months before my 25th birthday I had been experiencing quite a bit of pain in my left hip area, and wanted to get it thoroughly checked out. I had been working out with a personal trainer, so I thought I might have pulled a muscle or damaged a bone, or something along those lines. My doctor sent me for x-rays and an ultrasound, but nothing had showed up. I then was sent to a physiotherapist and was given exercises to do, but couldn't manage them because of the pain. The physiotherapist recommended that I get an MRI done, so I booked in for one on the first day I had free, which just happened to be my 25th birthday. (A word of advice – never get a scan on your birthday!) A few days before the scheduled scan I was in so much pain that I could barely move, and I knew something was seriously amiss.

Mum and I went to the hospital that birthday morning. When my name eventually was called, I walked through the door and prepared myself for what was to come. Little did I know, the result was going to mark the start of a new hurricane in my life. Normally an MRI takes about 15 minutes to about half an hour. After I had been in the machine for longer than that, I started to worry. About halfway through the scan, the radiologist pulled me out and said, 'We have found a lump.' The words stabbed me like a sharp knife. I was in shock, although part of me was relieved that they had found something, and I tried not to overreact.

The radiologist gave me an injection of dye, and I went back in for another hour or so. It felt like the longest time of my life. All the time I was lying on the bed, I kept hearing those words, 'We have found a lump,' echoing in my head. My face felt wet with silent tears. But I quickly brushed them away, refusing to acknowledge the severity of the situation.

Meanwhile, outside in the waiting room, Mum was worried because I had been in for so long. By now she guessed there must be something seriously wrong. She kept asking questions at the front desk, but they couldn't tell her anything; instead they tried to keep her calm. After I eventually came out she could tell by my face that there was something serious going on. The receptionist eventually handed me my scans, and sent a copy to my doctor that same day. Mum and I returned home in shock, hoping that it wasn't as bad as we thought it was.

A few hours later I received a call from my doctor's rooms saying that he wanted to see me that day and that it was urgent. Usually he was booked up far in advance, and you had to wait a long time before getting an appointment – so I knew that something was seriously wrong with me.

SILENCE IN THE DOCTOR'S OFFICE

As Mum and I entered the waiting room, we noticed that there were four other people waiting ahead of us. But as soon as the doctor appeared, he ushered us into his room. He closed the door behind us. There was a bit of a silence, which made the tension in the room even more obvious. He eventually spoke: 'The MRI results show a 7cm tumour which looks pretty nasty, and I'm pretty certain it is cancerous.' The words 'cancer' and 'tumour' echoed in my head repetitively.

The doctor then told me that my case was urgent, and that he needed to refer me to a surgeon for further help. As he was on the phone to the surgeon making the appointment, Mum and I looked at each other in the realisation that an intense storm had just hit, and we started crying silently. He was very apologetic for not having sent me for an MRI earlier (a tumour does not show up properly on x-ray or ultrasound). I told him not to blame himself, and thanked him for all he had done.

When I told my family the news they were hugely sympathetic, and encouraged me by saying that we would all get through this together. The appointment with the surgeon was for the following day. This time Dad came along too. Having to wait in the surgeon's waiting room for at least an hour only made the anticipation and fear even more unbearable. Eventually we were called in. He had a look at my scans; he then did an examination of my hip area and asked various questions, before asking me to take a seat. Then, for the longest ten seconds of my life, he looked me directly in the face, saying nothing. The words that followed shattered my world. He said, 'This is not good.'

At that moment time froze. Nothing else mattered. I could feel my eyes slowly filling with tears, but once again I fought back; I felt like I needed to be strong for my parents. He also told me that the worst-case scenario would be the possibility of losing my leg. When I heard this, I felt like my life was at a standstill. I immediately imagined myself in a wheelchair or with a prosthetic leg. It was hard to picture my life past that.

The surgeon told us that, based on my scans, he was very certain that the tumour was cancerous, and therefore I was an urgent case. He wanted to refer me to another surgeon, and booked me in for an appointment two days later. We thanked him and left. It was a very long and silent walk back to the car. I allowed some tears to come, but managed to contain most of them. The drive home was filled with silence, until I broke it by telling my parents something that they were not prepared for. I said that if in the middle of surgery the surgeon needed to amputate my leg, I gave them permission to say 'yes'. It was such a hard thing for me to say, but I knew that it needed to be addressed because of the severity of the situation. Once again, upon getting home I updated the rest of my family, and they assured me they would be with me every step of the way, no matter how far away some of them lived.

This whole experience felt like a bad dream that was happening to someone else. The full reality of this storm had not yet hit me. I kept thinking, 'Is this really happening to me?' The only time it felt real was when I felt pain or looked at my scan again to see the seven-centimetre potato-shaped tumour in my body. It was huge. The reason why it was causing me pain was because it was sitting directly on a nerve. It was weird to think that this tumour was inside me. I kept looking at my upper thigh in desperation, and willing it out.

GOD IS ALWAYS AT WORK

All of this made me angry with God. I didn't feel He was with me. He seemed so silent, now when I needed Him most. I was booked in to see my new surgeon at 4:30pm two days later. This was the earliest he could see me. My parents wanted to come along with me, but it was too late for them because Mum worked the night shift. I kept on praying (even though I felt that God was silent) that there would be a cancellation and we would be able to get in earlier. About one hour later I received a call from the receptionist to say that a 1pm appointment was now available. All I could now say was, 'Wow, God, you *are* listening.' This was the first time I had felt God's presence in a while. Everything had been so foggy up to then. Now it felt like it was starting to clear.

Before I knew it, two days had gone by, and we were about to meet the next surgeon. One of my parents' worries was finding parking in the city, since we were not very familiar with the area. But I prayed and believed that God had a bay reserved just for us in the car park. The receptionist had told me that if the number at the entrance of the car park read 000, then that meant that there were no spots left and we would have to find somewhere else. Well, when we arrived the number read 001. There was one spot left, and I knew that God had saved it for us! Once again God had heard and answered my prayer, even in such a little thing.

Sometimes when it doesn't seem that God is working in

your life, He is busy behind the scenes, where you can't see Him. Think of it as a stage performance, with God as the director as well as the backstage lights operator and cameraman. You can't see Him, but He makes sure that everything works and is in the right place at the right time. The show goes on, and He is in control.

MY LITTLE POTATO

Once we had found parking, located the floor we had to be on and reached the rooms, we still had to play the long waiting game. It felt like hours, and it was one of the most uncomfortable times of my life. I couldn't sit, so I had to keep moving around or lie down. Eventually, after an hour of waiting, we were finally called in. This long wait made me realise that this surgeon was not rushing, which meant he probably took time with and cared about every one of his patients. This gave me hope. When we finally met, we found him to be light-hearted and positive, which was exactly what we needed at this uncertain time. My tumour looked like a potato, so I had been calling it 'my little potato'. The surgeon thought it looked more like a pear, so we joked about that. That was the first time I had laughed since it had been discovered. Another thing I liked about him was that he gave us hope by saying that he believed that the tumour was benign. Now *that* was something really good to hear. However, in order to know precisely, a biopsy needed to be done. He booked me in for one in the following week. This would be the next step in my journey through this storm.

Before they could do the biopsy, I needed to get four tests done. We were able to book the blood test, chest x-ray and CT scan for that same day. I first had the blood test done.

Next was the chest X-ray, which was up on the next level. Whilst giving the receptionist my details, I started to feel dizzy. My sight and hearing started fading, and I began feeling so light-headed that I nearly passed out. I began having trouble with my breathing, and then started wheezing. By now I was struggling to keep talking. Eventually I couldn't stand anymore, and had to take a seat. Everyone around me was looking at me. It was so embarrassing, but all I could do was focus on my breathing. It turned out that because I hadn't eaten that whole day (in case they might need to do more scans) I had very low sugar levels. So one of the nurses kindly brought me an orange juice and some biscuits, and almost instantly I was myself again.

Once this was over, the nurse took me to the back room for the X-ray. Then I was led to another room to have the CT scan. My veins are very thin, so getting a needle in is always a challenge. I hate needles, but over the past few years I have become so used to them. This time the nurse couldn't find a vein, so I had to wait ten minutes for them to find a doctor to do it. After a few minutes of searching he found one, and injected the dye in. After the scan I met my parents back in the waiting room and we were ready to call it a day. It had been such an eventful and exhausting time for all of us.

The next morning Dad and I went back to the hospital to get the last test done. This time it was a PET scan, something that I had never experienced before. I had done some research on it the night before, and as a result of my findings had started to 'freak out' a bit. Upon arrival I was ushered into a room and told what was going to be done. They then checked my blood-sugar levels, which were fine. Then they attempted to put a cannula in my hand, which once again proved challenging. It was made harder still because I hadn't had anything to eat or drink since the night before, as I had been instructed.

They tried twice to insert the tube, but both attempts were unsuccessful. It was so painful that I began to cry. Dad had to walk out because he couldn't bear seeing this happening to me. I had to wait another fifteen to twenty minutes for a doctor to come and insert the cannula. He too was unsuccessful on the first few attempts. By this time I was in so much pain that I wanted to throw the doctor across the room. I know this sounds extreme, but the pain was unbearable and I just wanted to get away. Finally, on the fourth attempt, he managed to find a vein that was co-operative, and they injected a radioactive liquid into my veins. I was then escorted to a room and told to lie down on a bed and not move or talk. I had to lie as still as I could. I actually caught up on some sleep, which was great. Every twenty minutes they would come in and give me a liquid to drink. This apparently would help improve the definition of the scan. After an hour I was ready for the scan, and had to lie down on a table that moved backwards and forwards every few minutes while a scanner took various snapshots of my body. This took over thirty minutes, and once again I used the time to catch up on some sleep.

A few days later my parents and I met with the surgeon, who told us that the results from the scan were all clear. Praise God! I was over the moon. I was told that there was no cancer in the rest of my body. All I now needed was to have the biopsy, which would determine if the tumour was cancerous or not.

PRAYER IS POWERFUL

At this point I started asking more people to pray for me. I didn't know it at the time, but people all over the world were doing just that. When I found this out, all I could think was, 'Who am I that hundreds of people are praying for me?' I felt very loved and special, especially with all of the flowers, gifts and words of encouragement that I received. It really helped me so much, and I didn't feel nearly so alone anymore. And even more importantly, God was really starting to 'show up' again, even in the really little things.

I have seen amazing answers to prayer. With my very own eyes I have seen people healed. I have also seen people who were very far away from God turn back to Him and commit their lives to Him again. I have seen the impossible made possible. So I *know* that prayer works. No matter what happens in your life, always pray – because He is listening and He cares about you. He will never leave you.

'X' MARKS THE SPOT

Before I knew it, one week had come and gone, and I was back in hospital, signing in for my overnight stay. The anxiety that I was feeling at that moment was almost suffocating. I felt that nothing could calm my fears. Mum and my sister waited with me until it was time for me to go in. I said my goodbyes, and embarked on the next step of the journey alone. Well, not completely alone – I had God with me every step of the way, of course.

There I was, dressed in my hospital gown and ready to be wheeled into theatre to have surgery that could radically change the rest of my life. It was a scary thought. I was supposed to be in theatre at 11am, and it was now nearly 12:30pm. The waiting was absolutely killing me. Finally my surgeon made an appearance. He barely spoke to me, and marked an 'X' on my left thigh, exactly where he was going to do the biopsy. He then disappeared through the theatre doors, which kept opening directly in front of me. Every time they opened I became more anxious to get it over and done with. Finally the anaesthetist inserted the cannula into my hand and started administering the anaesthetic. I started to feel very relaxed, and everything around me started fading. I was wheeled into the operating theatre. All I remember seeing was my surgeon all gowned up and looking at my MRI scans on the screen, and then I was out cold.

The biopsy involved making a small incision and removing a sample of the tumour in order to examine it more closely and thereby determine if it was benign or malignant. Apparently I took a while to wake up, but when I eventually did I remember two nurses bending over me asking questions. I could barely answer and just kept falling back asleep. I tried to shift myself, but pain struck instantly. This was the first time I had ever woken up from surgery in pain. I realised that this was because the tumour was still pushing against a nerve. The next minute I remember being wheeled around into an elevator and then into my hospital room. Then, best of all, I remember seeing Mum and my sister, and I didn't feel alone anymore.

Once I was settled in they left, seeing as I was only staying overnight. I felt hugely relieved that the biopsy was over. Now it was just about waiting for the results to come in. I'm so glad that prayer does not run out or have a shelf life – because I would have exceeded my limit with the number of times I prayed for that tumour to be benign.

I will now tell you something amazing. I woke up at home one morning before my surgery, and I distinctly heard 'someone' whisper in my ear very clearly, 'It's benign.' I believe that was God reassuring me that the tumour was not cancerous. After I heard this all fear left me, and I knew God's perfect love and comfort. Those words were my hope and anchor, reminding me that God already knew the results. Also, I had so many people praying from me, many of whom heard from God that it was going to be benign.

I want to reassure you that you can handle more than you think you can. Remember that. If you are going through a really painful storm right now, I want to encourage you to keep pushing through it. You might feel like you are drowning or that the storm is too strong to overcome. I promise you, your storm will never overcome you, unless you let it. Our God is bigger than any storm you could ever face. Remember that He is always working behind the scenes for the good of those who love him. You need not fear because He is with you. He will get you through whatever you are facing. Just keep on praying.

LET'S SAY A PRAYER

Lord, I pray for the storm that I am currently facing. I know that you are with me, and that you will not let it overcome me. I know that this is just a season that will eventually pass. I am an overcomer in Christ. Lord, I know that you will give me strength and help me to persevere until the storm calms. Help me not to fear but rather to stay positive. In Jesus' name I pray. Amen.

CHAPTER REVIEW

- God is always working behind the scenes.
- Prayer doesn't have a shelf life or limit.
- You can handle more than you think you can.
- Never give up.
- Unless you let it, the storm will never overcome you.
- This is just a season – it will pass.

Chapter 11
THE AFTERMATH

> I will praise the Lord no matter what happens. I will constantly speak of his glories and grace. I will boast of all his kindness to me. Let all who are discouraged take heart. Let us praise the Lord together and exalt his name.
>
> Psalm 34:1-3 TLB

The next week I went to see my surgeon to receive my results. I remember that whole week so clearly as I waited anxiously to find out if the tumour was benign or not. I once even called up the receptionist hoping for news, but she told me that even though they had received the results she couldn't discuss them over the phone with me. That made me even more anxious.

Finally the time for my appointment arrived, and I walked in, my parents by my side. When we had all sat down, the first thing the surgeon said was, 'The results have come back and it is benign.' I cannot explain the weight that lifted off my shoulders when I heard those words. Even though God had already told me all would be well, it was great to hear that confirmation.

So now that step one had been completed, it was time

to get step two out of the way. I was hoping he could do the surgery that week. However, because he was going away on holiday, the earliest he could fit me in was in one month's time. When I heard that, I was really disappointed. I was in so much pain from the biopsy and the tumour was still pressing on a nerve. I wanted it all to end. But all I could do was to wait patiently and count the days until my scheduled surgery. My family felt that one month went by quickly, but to me it felt like forever.

My surgeon explained to me the process that was going to take place. They would make an incision from my left hip joint to halfway down my left leg, remove the tumour, stitch it all up, and then put in a tube that would slowly drain out the excess blood. I would have to remain in hospital until it was fully drained. The thing that concerned me the most was the tube in my leg. How would that eventually be removed? Would it hurt?

A few days before surgery I became very fearful. I started to cry out to God, asking Him to heal me *before* my surgery, so I wouldn't have to proceed with it. Here is an excerpt from my journal, written the night before I was due to go in. It shows how much anxiety I was experiencing, and how much I did not want to go through with it.

Lord please heal me. Take this tumour away. I don't want to have this surgery. I'm really scared. I don't want to do this. I don't want to go through this. It's a huge cut. I can't even cry because I feel like I will have a panic attack.

I need to focus and stay calm. Breathe in, breathe out. I know you are here Lord with me. I feel your presence. Be with me Lord. I need you. Draw close to me. I can't do this alone. I know you are always there for me.

The Aftermath

If there is any other way... Lord please take this away. I do not want to go through with this.

But ... if it is your will then let it be done.

I now want to tell you a true story, one which at the time really inspired me. It's found in the Old Testament, in the book of Daniel. There were three guys living in Babylon – Shadrach, Meshach and Abednego. At that time King Nebuchadnezzar built a huge golden image and commanded that everyone bow down to it when they heard sound of musical instruments being played. These three guys only worshipped the one true Living God, so they refused to follow this command. They would *not* bow down to this golden image. This made the king furious, and he decided to throw them into a blazing furnace in punishment. Listen to their inspiring response:

> Shadrach, Meshach and Abednego replied to him, 'King Nebuchadnezzar, we do not need to defend ourselves before you in this matter. If we are thrown into the blazing furnace, the God we serve is able to deliver us from it, and he will deliver us from Your Majesty's hand. But *even if he does not*, we want you to know, Your Majesty, that we will not serve your God or worship the image of gold you have set up.'
>
> Daniel 3:16-20

I want to highlight the words 'even if he does not'. They demonstrate these three men's obedience to God – they were willing to die in that blazing furnace rather than bow down to the king's idol. They knew that God *could* save them, but they were prepared to die if He didn't. Nothing would stop them from obeying God. How amazing is their faith?

That was my same attitude before having the surgery. I knew that if God wanted to heal me, He could – for nothing is impossible with Him. But even if he didn't, I would still trust in Him and worship Him.

GOODBYE, MY LITTLE POTATO

From the time the tumour was discovered to the time it was removed, the days dragged by. Every day I would look at my leg and tell the tumour to 'get out'. I experienced so many different emotions throughout that long month of waiting. On the one hand I felt positive because I knew it wasn't cancerous; but on the other hand I felt frustrated because I had waited so long and wanted it over and done with. I was also nervous because the operation was going to take over two hours, and I had never before experienced such a long time in surgery.

After a month of anxiously waiting, the day finally arrived. The operation was scheduled for 9:30am. Mum, Dad and I were up nice and early to ensure we would have enough time to drive there and arrive one hour early, so I could be signed in and ready well before time. Upon walking in, I found everything the same as the last time. The same smells, the same sounds, the same sign in the room, the same coloured gown, the same nurse. The only thing that was different this time was that my family were allowed to stay with me while I waited to go into the operating theatre. I was delighted about this, and it made me feel less alone.

They gave me a blood test and then took me to the same room and to exactly the same bed I had been in for the biopsy. All the memories from the month before came flooding back into my mind. The same anaesthetist appeared and put the cannula into my hand. After he injected the sedative I said goodbye to my parents as I was being wheeled away. I started feeling drowsy and numb, just like I had before my biopsy. I was taken into the same operating theatre as the last time. I mumbled something incoherent to my surgeon. I was aware of nurses helping lift me off the bed and onto the operating table next to it. The last thing I remember was having a mask placed over my face and the gas slowly putting me to sleep. As I faded away, all I could think was, 'Goodbye, my little potato.'

IT IS FINISHED
When I woke up hours later one of the nurses was with me, checking my charts and attending to me. Once again I found it difficult to stay awake, and kept falling back into sleep. Then I was wheeled into the ward and saw my parents waiting for me. I was bursting with excitement at seeing them, but still felt drowsy. I remember my throat feeling so dry that I could barely speak. But they didn't need me to speak; we were all just so relieved it was over. They could tell I needed to rest, so they stayed for a while and then left.

The next day a physiotherapist arrived to help me with my walking. I struggled to put weight on my left foot. As soon as I tried to stand, I collapsed straight onto the floor. The physiotherapist had to pick me up and put me back on my bed. I couldn't walk, and it felt so overwhelming that I nearly had a panic attack. But slowly I gained feeling back in the leg. And although I initially started walking with a limp, I was soon moving perfectly up and down the corridors. In a few days I was even walking up and down stairs. It felt great to be out of my hospital bed. The nurses couldn't believe how quickly I was walking around.

Every morning that I was there they would inject a needle into my thigh to prevent a blood clot forming. That stung for ten minutes, and was the longest ten minutes of my life. I never looked forward to waking up in the morning at the hospital because I knew what was going to happen.

Every time I wanted to go to the bathroom I had to take two bags with me. Both were connected via a tube to my thigh, one to drain the blood, the other for pain relief. If the pain became too much for me, I could press a button and an analgesic would automatically be injected. Thankfully, I never once had to use it.

The worst thing I had to contend with whilst there was the continual nausea. I couldn't eat or drink anything. The nurses had to pump fluids into me, just to keep me going. It stopped only on the last day there.

There was one other complication. I had two cannulas in my right arm – one was being utilised and the other was just a backup. One night when I was ready to go to sleep, I became aware that my drip was stinging. I buzzed for one of the nurses to check it, and she found that the cannula had come out of my vein and it was pumping fluid into my hand instead. This is the reason why it was stinging. The cannula was quickly removed and the tube was swapped over to my backup cannula. Once again I was ready to settle in and go to sleep, when my backup cannula started to sting. I turned on my light and had a look at it myself before calling one of the nurses. The same thing had happened. They then had to remove my backup cannula as well, and it was just about midnight by the time they inserted a brand-new cannula into my left arm (because my right arm was so bruised). So, in the space of less than half an hour, I had two cannulas removed and one new one inserted. I have already told you about my fear of needles, especially cannulas. I think this forced me to face this fear and in some measure overcome it.

I never felt lonely once during that time as there were so many visitors and gifts, all of which I appreciated so much. Also, I had a room-mate with whom I bonded really well . We were able to support and encourage each other through the tough days as well as celebrate each other's victories. I was glad to be able to encourage her when she started walking again.

Every morning the surgeon would visit the ward to check on his patients. Every time he saw me he gave me a better report. I was supposed to stay in hospital for nearly a week but, seeing as I had improved so quickly, I was discharged after just four days. It was the best thing in the world to hear I could finally go home. No more stinging needles in my thigh every morning, no more carrying two bags when I needed to go to the bathroom, and no more early wake-up calls. I was finally free... though not just yet.

Being discharged took a little bit longer than expected. I thought I would just sign a few pages and then leave. However, I had forgotten the two tubes that were still in my leg. The first tube came out very quickly because it was just there for pain relief. The second tube, however, was coiled up in my thigh, so it took quite a long time to remove. To help this out, the nurse told me to keep coughing out loud really hard. As I coughed she started to pull. I felt every centimetre of it as it emerged. It was a very uncomfortable experience, but thankfully over quickly. The nurse then replaced my bandages and finally discharged me.

LET'S SAY A PRAYER

Lord, I pray that through every season, whether it be harvest time or winter, I will praise you and exalt your name. You are worthy to be praised. I pray that no matter what pain I experience, I will remember that you are in the boat sailing through the storm with me. I pray that, whether or not I receive healing, I will continue to worship you. This I pray in Jesus' name. Amen.

CHAPTER REVIEW

- Storms allow you to face your fears.
- Even if you don't receive healing, still keep worshipping God.
- God is in everything with you.

Chapter 12
WHEN YOUR STORMS BECOME A SHADOW

> I have fought the good fight, I have finished the race, I have kept the faith.
>
> 2 Timothy 4:7

It was near the end of a long and stressful year when I visited my surgeon for my first follow-up consultation after the biopsy and the successful surgery to remove my tumour. He told me that I could expect to experience nerve pain for up to a full *year*. I had known there would be some residual pain, but had only expected this to last a few weeks. Now it felt like my whole new year was about to be ruined, and I had nothing to look forward to except pain, *again*. Just when I thought it was over, it now seemed there was more to follow.

Let me explain to you what my nerve pain felt like. At times it felt like there were random electric shocks exploding inside my leg. At other times it felt like a knife was ripping layers of skin off. And yet at other times it felt like my leg was open and exposed, but at the same time very numb and tingly; this was a weird sensation, one that is hard to describe. I had been looking forward to the new year in the hopes of a fresh new start, but it now seemed the my storm was following me like a long, long shadow.

Hope in the Storms

When Jesus died on the cross for you, He took it *all*. He took all your sin, all your shame, all your burdens and sorrows, all your guilt and all your sickness. He doesn't want you carrying these burdens around, not even one of them, not even for only one day. He wants you to throw them off, and give them to Him. They are all unnecessary weight that will limit you and restrict you. *Just like me.* I felt that I was forced to drag my storm with me into the new year. *But that was totally unnecessary.*

> Therefore, since we are surrounded by such a great cloud of witnesses, let us throw off everything that hinders and the sin that so easily entangles, and let us run with perseverance the race marked out for us. Let us fix our eyes on Jesus, the author and perfecter of our faith, who for the joy set before him endured the cross, scorning its shame, and sat down at the right hand of the throne of God.
>
> Hebrews 12:1–2

The verses above talk about running the race of life, and how to do so successfully. Now imagine running a race carrying an empty backpack. It's easy, right? But what happens if every time you encounter a problem or a burden, a brick gets added to this backpack. Soon it's going to be so heavy you won't be able to run the race anymore. You will start to jog, then maybe walk, and eventually you will not be able to even stand up. You will be crawling on the ground, still trying to struggle on.

Throw off the backpack. Keep running with perseverance. Don't look back. Look forward to *Jesus*. He is standing at the finishing line, waiting for you. I'm not saying that this will make you immune to trials; they will still occur in your life. But Jesus doesn't want you to carry these burdens that hinder you. So *don't* run with them; rather throw them off. He wants you to live a life of freedom. *He tells us to cast them on Him* instead (see 1 Peter 5:7). What an amazing offer! Don't turn it down.

RECOVERY

I wish I could tell you that recovery is easy. But, unfortunately, it never is. No matter what physical setback or emotional trauma you have gone through, recovery is always a *process* of slowly getting back on your feet again. It's one small step at a time, in the right direction, through the pain. The healing process takes time.

In my case, recovery was very painful. As the surgery involved removing the tumour off a nerve, I was left with chronic nerve pain in my left thigh, which was very debilitating. Quite apart from the pain, I also struggled with people not being able to understand what I was going through. They supported me and prayed for me, but never really understood exactly what I was experiencing. Since the tumour was gone, it was hard for them to understand that I was still in pain.

I remember that the first few days back at home it was very painful for me to walk around. I lived with my parents in a two-storey house. I went straight upstairs upon coming home from hospital, and for the next few days I lived upstairs in my room, and couldn't go downstairs at all. I missed eating and socialising downstairs with my family. I missed going outside into the sun. But I knew the most important thing for me was rest.

I'm the type of person who finds it difficult to sit around and do nothing; I need to be always doing something. So, lying in bed for two weeks was not easy for me. I was very bored and I felt so lazy, and the constant pain didn't assist matters at all.

Many people came to visit, some thoughtfully bringing little activities for me to do whilst I rested in bed.

For the first two days after arriving home there was a tingling sensation and numbness in my left thigh which was so intense that I began to fear I was losing all feeling in it. It was very unpleasant. I was so concerned that I rang my surgeon. He told me that this was the nerve pain he had warned me about, and that I should expect it to last for 12 months. I was shocked when I heard this. All I wanted to do was crawl into a hole and go to sleep until it was over. I know this sounds like I'm exaggerating, but I was really distressed, and just wanted to give up. If I couldn't handle two days of this heavy, numbing sensation in my thigh, how would I survive a whole year of it?

I want you to know that this was just my initial reaction to the shock of the situation. Once I had spent time with God, I started to believe once again that He could heal me, and that my recovery time would be much shorter. I started drawing closer to Him and trusting in Him once again – and He gave my heart the assurance that He *would* get me through this, just as He had with everything else.

I want to encourage you to trust God *straight away* when bad news hits. It's hard, I know, and I'm still learning to do it myself. But if you do, it immediately changes the situation. God is waiting to intervene *as soon as we ask Him*. It's simply crazy not to ask Him for help. If we don't trust God, we often end up being angry with Him and the world, and becoming depressed very easily. Try to be led by your spirit, not by your flesh. Try to be led by the voice of Truth, not by the voice of deception – that voice in your head telling you that God either doesn't care or is not able to intervene. Try to stay positive by thinking positively.

During the last few months of my recovery my leg became extremely painful. Some days it felt that, with each step I took, it was going to fall off. On other days it felt like the skin on my thigh was being peeled off with a knife. Yet on other days there would be no pain at all. Every day was different. Nothing during this recovery process was consistent or predictable.

How did I get through this time? I took it one day at a time. I took it one step at a time. Yes, it was painful, but I stayed positive and focused my energy on writing this book instead of dwelling on the pain. I had amazing support around me. I had many people praying for me. I had God on my side, and I trusted Him. I could see the finishing line!

ANNIVERSARIES

I finally reached the one-year anniversary of the removal of my tumour, when I had finally said goodbye to it, and it felt unreal. When I looked back at all I had gone through, the whole experience seemed something hard to grasp. I was so proud of myself for making it this far, and realised how strong I had been. Even though the tumour had knocked me down, I had been able to get back up and keep fighting.

I honestly thought the year of recovery would drag on (and trust me, during the painful days it definitely did), but suddenly it was over. I can now look back at the experience and see that I have grown because of it. In that period nothing defeated me. I know that it was not in my own strength, but rather in God's, that I had made it through each painful day. Some people thought that after my surgery my recovery would be quick, and couldn't understand why I was still in pain one year on. It was hard for them to believe the extent of the pain.

Sometimes I felt that they thought I was making excuses. But I wasn't. It was definitely less painful than it has been in the beginning of that recovery year, but there were still days that were unbearable. Nonetheless, when I finally reached the end of that year, I couldn't believe it had passed so quickly.

You may have reached your one-year anniversary of a difficult storm, or are coming up to that time. Well, I would like to congratulate you. Well done. You made it (or have nearly made it, and have not got too far to go). Look back and see the new strength that you now have. See the changes that have taken place. You are not the same person. Don't let anything ever defeat you. Continue to stand strong. Continue to persevere. *Continue to have faith and hope in God.*

REFINEMENT

As that year came to an end, my pain was nearly gone. The new year looked like a promising one to me, and everything was starting to go well again. I was planning to find a new job. I was in a new relationship, and we were planning to find a new church together. Everything seemed fresh and new.

But when in January of that new year my boyfriend and I broke up, my world came crashing down. At the same time I was very ill with a gastro virus (which I talk about in Chapter 13). A domino-effect ensued, and I started feeling that my life was collapsing. Everyone around me was telling me, 'Be strong,' and 'You have been through worse.' But these words were unhelpful to me at that time. I felt like I was in quicksand, and every new word of 'encouragement' just made me sink deeper in; I simply couldn't bear to hear them. At one point I felt like I was so deep in that I couldn't escape. I felt lost; I felt empty; I felt hopeless.

As you already know, the title of this book is *Hope in the Storms*. Well, when I was experiencing this next storm, I lost most of my hope. I could feel it slowly draining away. I even struggled to continue writing this book, because I couldn't *feel* any hope at all. I kept thinking, 'How can I encourage others to have hope in their storm, when I can't even have hope in my own personal storm?' This made me think long and hard about life.

It is so easy to have hope in God when everything in your life is going well; when you have a stable job, a healthy family, supportive friends, an amazing church family, and everything else you need. But what about when negative things happen in your life? You lose your job, your relationship ends, your family or friends get sick or abandon you, and you don't feel God's presence any more in your life. What then?

I believe that God often uses storms as a *refinement process* in our lives. Let's use the analogy of gold. Gold as it is when it has just been mined, is unworkable; it needs to first be refined. Part of that refining process is 'smelting' (melting) it in a fiery furnace, so that the alloys (impure elements mixed in) can be separated off. Only then is it strong enough and pliable enough to be shaped into something useful or beautiful.

Think of your painful storms as that fiery furnace. Whilst in it, you probably think you are going to be burnt up and that you won't survive. But if you have God *with you in there*, just like Shadrach, Meshach and Abednego did (refer back to their story in Chapter 12), you will *not* be defeated, *nor* will you be destroyed. Just as once that gold has been removed from the furnace and goes through a process whereby all the impurities are removed, so too with our lives.

Jesus has already died for all of our iniquities and sins *if we believe in Him and come to him for forgiveness*. But we still need to go through the refinement process, to allow those things that hinder our growth and wellbeing to be removed.

One day I was on my bed crying out to God, asking Him why He was allowing all this to happen to me. I was at such a low point that I felt like I couldn't escape the depression I was feeling. Then suddenly God revealed why I was going through all of this. He told me it was so that I could write a book that would change other people's lives and encourage them in ways never known before. It finally all made sense – why all this opposition was coming my way. Because the enemy was not happy with what I was doing, and wanted to throw obstacles in my path. Well, I said, 'Bring it on. Nothing will stop me from writing this book.' And so far, nothing has. I even told God, 'Even if I lose my arms, legs or sight while writing this book, I will find another way to complete it.' I know that sounds crazy, but that was the most extreme situation I could think of.

Have you ever heard about a man named Jean-Dominique Bauby, who wrote an entire book by blinking with one eye? He had suffered a massive stroke, which only allowed him to move his left eyelid, but his mind was still 100 percent alert. He wrote his whole book by blinking to a scribe. It took about ten months and over 200,000 blinks to finish, but complete it he did. When you hear of stories like this, you ask yourself, 'What is stopping me from completing this?' If this guy can write a book by blinking with only one eyelid, then what is my excuse? He kept on going despite his physical disability. He wouldn't let a stroke stop his voice from being heard. He had a story to tell, and he told it. No matter how long it took him to complete, he persevered – and out of it came a book and the major movie *The Diving Bell and the Butterfly*.

END-DATE FOR YOUR STORM

Guess what? Whatever you are going through will not last forever. God has already set an end-date. Take hope – that end does exist. A few months after my tumour removal, I took on a very different attitude. I had just been through a downward spiral after the frustration of so many months of intense nerve pain. I began to change, so much so that even my friends and family noticed. I started swearing more often, and became angry and frustrated all the time. People kept saying to me, 'At least it wasn't cancer.' Yes, I was happy that the tumour was out of my body and that it hadn't been cancerous, but I was still suffering with chronic pain. I began pushing people away, and started losing friends because of it. This negative attitude lasted for a few weeks.

One Sunday I woke up in a lot of pain, and instead of going to church I stayed home in bed. I was crying out to God, asking him how I was supposed to deal with this pain. I said to Him, 'Yes I know it's not cancer, but there is still pain.' I then went on to YouTube and typed in 'preaching about pain'. 'Don't Let the Pain Hurt', a video by Joel Osteen, came up. I clicked on it, not knowing that what I was about to watch would change my perspective completely. Have you ever heard a message in which everything is 'spot on' for you, the perfect message for you at that time? Well, that's what happened to me that day. What I heard made me feel like a new person, and suddenly I had a new perspective on my life.

The first thing that really got my attention was Joel Osteen sharing the Bible verse which reads,

> **Even though I walk through the valley of the shadow of death, I will fear no evil.**
>
> Psalm 23:4 (ESV)

He then highlighted the word 'through'. He expanded on it by saying that you walk *through* the valley, you don't camp there. You are not stuck there. The valley is a temporary place in your journey. You might be there for a season, but God has already set an end-date to your suffering. Isn't that great to know?

Another thing he said was that when you go through suffering, don't just *go* through it, but rather *grow* through it. Whatever happens in your life, your attitude will either make you or break you. It's your choice as to how you want to react to the situation. God doesn't *send* bad things. But He will use the situation for the good of those who love Him. No one is exempt from problems. We all will walk through the valley at some point in our lives. God's perceived 'rejections' can sometimes be a *redirection* in life.

When you are walking through the dark valley, remember that you are not alone. Jesus is with you. He is your Shepherd. You are his sheep. Listen to your Shepherd's voice so that He can guide you safely through the danger. He will give you the strength and peace that you need in order to get through the valley safely, to pass through the storm. No matter how stormy the seas are or how shaky the situation is, you have a solid *Saviour* (someone who saves you).

It says in the Bible that no matter what fire you go through, you shall not be burnt. Do you know why? Because God has his hands on the thermostat. He is controlling the temperature. He will never let it get too hot for you to handle. The enemy wants to destroy you. He would destroy you if he had control of the thermostat, but he doesn't have any control. God is in control of your life. I'm not saying that it's going to be an easy walk. It still will get very hot in the fire, but this is in preparation for the next level that God has planned for you. The next assignment that he wants you to fulfil is on the other side of that fiery furnace. Difficulties are a part of life. Remember, every struggle you experience is making you stronger.

THERE IS A REASON FOR THIS PAIN

Joel Osteen used the example of a pregnant woman, and what she experiences during those nine months of pregnancy. There may be nausea, discomfort, bleeding and sometimes even swelling. Her body is getting ready for a huge thing to take place. There is a purpose for this change – her body is getting ready to give birth to a brand-new baby; a beautiful new life is about to come into the world. So too with many things in life.

You can give birth to new ministries. You can reach new levels with God. But you have to be prepared for changes to first occur. Change starts with the promised seed being planted and then comes the growth, and with it the stretching. You have to be prepared for some hardships along the way. It's not an easy route, and there are no shortcuts.

You have to take the one path that will get you to your destination, and along the way you will have mountains to face. But just remember, climbing a mountain can be exhausting, and sometimes you may feel like you want to give up and turn back. However, if you concentrate on finally reaching the top and on the view you will have when you get there, it makes it worth all the trouble, discomfort and pain. It is such a huge achievement.

DON'T LET YOUR RESTRICTIONS RULE YOUR LIFE

There were so many times in my life, especially during my tumour experience, when I felt very restricted. Restricted physically. Restricted in what I could wear. Restricted in social events. Restricted in leisure activities. Restricted emotionally.

For example, after my ankle injury I was forced to wear sneakers with orthotics in them for two years. This took place over the time of my 21st birthday party, when I would have loved to dress up and wear high heels, but I wasn't able to. Instead I had to wear flats. However, I still made the most of my time – I still had fun and I made the night a memorable one.

Also, my ankle injury did not stop me from singing in the worship team on Sundays at church. I simply had to sit down on a chair whilst singing. Yes, I looked different, but I didn't care. It didn't affect my voice! Another time I attended a Christmas party, and the restaurant had a dance floor with great music, but I couldn't dance. If you knew me you'd know that I love to dance; I'm always the first person on the dance floor and the last person off. But nevertheless I managed to sing along to the songs and enjoy myself from my chair.

When I wanted to lose weight and get fit after my surgery, I couldn't even attempt it because of the risk of making my pain worse. But I stayed positive, and day by day slowly started seeing improvement through small exercises. Even though there were many restrictions that I faced through my storm, I still thought positively and tried changing the situation for the better whenever I could. I believe a positive attitude makes all the difference – and if you try it, you will be amazed at how many others you will inspire to do so too.

You may feel that you are being restricted in your situation because of your health or some other circumstance. How you fare comes down to your attitude. Stay positive and your storm will be tolerable. Throw off everything that is hindering you and weighing you down – give it to God. He doesn't want you to carry burdens around with you. All they do is weigh you down and cause you to drown. Give them to Him. Let the Lord be your strength and shield. Let the Lord be your joy in everything.

You may be going through something in your life that feels endless. But I can promise you that God has set an end-date to it. It's not going to last forever. It may be frustrating and restricting, but after the storm has cleared there will always be a rainbow of hope. *God makes everything beautiful in its time* (Ecclesiastes 3:11).

LET'S SAY A PRAYER

Lord, I pray that whenever I encounter a storm I will know and trust that you have already set an end-date to it. Lord, remind me that this storm will not last forever. I am only *passing through* this valley; I am not camping in it. I pray that I will know you are with me, and that you will be my comfort and strength during this time. Help me to block out *all* other voices except yours. Lord, I thank you that even though I may be shaken, I will not be destroyed – you are my Saviour, the solid rock on which I stand. I put my hope and trust in you. I pray all of this in Jesus' name. Amen.

CHAPTER REVIEW

- God will get you through the recovery process.
- Don't let pain restrict you.
- Fix your eyes on Jesus, and keep running the race.
- Jesus doesn't want you carrying around unnecessary weights in your life.
- God has set an end-date to your storm.
- Walk *through* the valley, don't camp there.
- Don't just *go* through the suffering, *grow* through it too.
- Pain happens because a change is taking place.
- Stay positive throughout your storm.

Chapter 13
MIRACLES DO HAPPEN

> Jesus looked at them and said, 'With man this is impossible, but with God all things are possible.'
> Matthew 19:26

Reflect on the following few questions before you read on. Do you believe in miracles? Do you believe that God can heal you? Do you believe that God can completely change your life? Well, not only do I *believe* that God can do these things, but I have personally experienced and witnessed all of them. They happened to me.

In Chapter 12 I talked about reaching the one-year anniversary of my tumour removal. I then had to get another MRI scan done to check for any recurrence. One week after the scan, I had a meeting booked with my surgeon in order to take the results back to him. It was about a two-hour drive in really bad traffic. The whole time going there I was praying that he would give me positive news. I was expecting my surgeon to say that there would be no more pain the following year, and that I didn't have to see him for another six months. These seemed entirely reasonable expectations ... or so I thought.

The hospital brought back so many memories of my stay

there. I smelt the same smells, saw the same nurses, and even got a look at the room that I stayed in for those four days. When I was called in to see my surgeon, he checked my leg for pain and measured how much it had healed. The good news was that it had healed 31cm, which was great. He had expected more than that, but was happy with the progress. I asked him if I would ever get full feeling back in my leg, and his reply was, 'Most likely never.' Let me explain to you what my leg felt like at this stage. It was numb because of nerve damage, and it was also tender to touch and often very painful. Nerve pain is really difficult to describe.

He then looked at my MRI scan and it was all clear. Praise God for that. He wanted me to come back in four months with another scan. I then asked him about the pain, and what I could expect in the future. He said that it probably would keep on travelling down past my knee, and that the following year would be another painful year for me. After hearing this news, I was really upset. I had wanted a fresh new beginning, one with no more pain or restrictions. Was that too much to ask for? Now I felt as if my pain was following me once again, like a shadow. I booked my next appointment with him and left the hospital.

On the drive home I felt numb. I didn't know what to think. Part of me felt like giving up; another part wanted to keep striving and pushing through. At the time I had an amazing friend, and I told him everything about the surgeon's meeting, and expressed how frustrated I was feeling. He prayed about what he could do for me, and God told him, 'Take Chantal to Prayer Mountain.' Prayer Mountain is a House of Prayer in Merroo, and it's absolutely beautiful. The presence of God in that place is so tangible and real. My friend asked me if I was free that Friday to attend the healing service there and, surprisingly, it was the only free Friday I had for a while – so I booked in without any hesitation. He drove me up to Prayer Mountain that Friday night. The week leading up to this I had been walking around with an expectant attitude, with faith that I would receive healing. About a month prior to this, this same friend had gone to Prayer Mountain himself with pain in his hand that he had experienced his whole life, and he had received healing for it that night. He was no longer in pain.

During the worship at the healing service my friend and I kept praying and expecting that I would receive healing. We believed that a miracle was going to take place in my life that night. I was standing up when the pastor approached me. She asked me what I needed prayer for. I told her my situation, and that my surgeon had told me I would never receive feeling back in my leg. She told everyone in the room to stretch out their hands towards me and start praying.

The moment she started praying and placing her hands on my head, my entire left leg went numb. I couldn't feel it at all. I lost my balance a little, but I had my friend next to me holding me so that I wouldn't fall. I kept stamping my left foot in an attempt to get the feeling back, but it remained completely numb. Then it felt as if a covering had been placed over my entire left leg, as if it was being protected. It felt like I was wearing armour on it. Then, out of nowhere, it started shaking uncontrollably. The power of God was all over my leg. I couldn't control it. I just flowed with what the Holy Spirit was doing, and I kept saying, 'I receive this healing in Jesus' name.' This continued for about five minutes.

After prayer I had to sit down. My leg felt heavy and numb,

and I couldn't really walk on it properly. After I returned to my seat I started kicking my leg and stretching it out, just to see if I could feel it; but I still had no feeling. But I wasn't worried. I knew what I had felt, and I knew that God had healed me. I was expectant. I had received the healing and kept on thanking God for it. When the pastor had finished praying for my leg, she had said that the enemy was going to regret that he had ever tried to mess with me, and she was right. I waited a bit longer to see if my leg would get feeling back, but it didn't. My friend had to walk me back to the car, with me leaning completely on him. He drove me back home and walked me to my door to make sure I got home safely.

The next day I woke up and my leg was still very heavy and numb. But by lunchtime I could walk perfectly well, and I had no pain at all! I had been walking around thanking God and receiving His healing for my leg, and he had honoured this. I now was free! That night Mum and I were booked into a hotel which had an outdoor heated pool. Up to now I had barely even been able to walk in the water because it had caused too much strain on my leg. However, this time I was able to do laps without any pain at all. I continually praised God for healing me.

That same night at the hotel I woke up with excruciating pain in my leg, about ten times the level I normally would experience. It was awful, and I couldn't sleep. But instead of letting doubt creep into my mind about not being healed completely, I grabbed my leg and started saying, 'I receive the healing, Jesus. I am healed in Jesus' name. I thank you for the healing.' After about five minutes, the pain vanished. That was the last time I *ever* felt any pain in my left leg. To this day I thank God for healing me. I will never forget it.

I always find that once you have experienced something incredible like this, you have to share it with others. So I started telling people about my healing. Some people were amazed, others were shocked, and yet others didn't believe me.

One person I particularly wanted to share this news with was my surgeon. He was a non-believer. So the next time I went to see him with my new MRI results, I walked in with such confidence and joy that he could see the difference in my face.

He asked the usual questions about the pain, the recovery and the medication dosage. But when I told him that I had no pain, that I didn't have to take my medication anymore and that God had healed me, he froze. He then told me of another incident he had either witnessed or heard of, of a lady who had had cancer, and how God had healed her too. It looked like he was pondering these stories and trying to come up with an answer, but just couldn't.

I told him, before even looking at the scans, that the MRI results would be clear. He took out the scans, looked at them, and was shocked when he saw I was correct. He then did the usual checking of my leg to test where the nerve pain was. When I told him I had full feeling back in my leg (minus a few centimetres at the top), he once again looked surprised. It was quite humorous, seeing the look on his face. I told him that miracles *do* happen, and that this was one of them. It was the best session I'd had with him, by far. Normally I would have had to see him every three months, and then it would go to six-monthly check-ups. Now he had changed it to me seeing him once a year!

WHAT NEXT?

After I received the healing from my nerve pain, there wasn't even two weeks of freedom before my next storm hit. I now had to battle a pretty nasty gastro virus, which made me feel nauseous, light-headed, dizzy and extremely weak. Do you see what I mean when I say I'm seldom without pain of some sort? I couldn't even enjoy a little bit of freedom from nerve pain without something else creeping up on me. During this gastro virus I had lost about five kilos because I couldn't eat. I had wanted to lose weight anyway, but certainly not this way.

Having this virus also meant I missed out on numerous events. I was supposed to have a karaoke evening with my best friend and her siblings, as well as have a sleepover at their place, but I was too sick. At the same time a friend had her final music performance in the city, but I couldn't make it because I was too weak. I had been praying with her about her performance for a long time, so when I had to miss it, I was devastated. Another friend was celebrating the opening of his business and I had been invited to attend, but I missed that too because I was too dizzy. Yet another friend's wedding was approaching, and I told myself, 'I will be better by that day.' But I missed it.

I was devastated; I was frustrated; I was angry with God once again. I remember watching my family getting dressed up for this friend's wedding, while I sat there in my PJs, upset. It was very difficult. I walked around the house crying the entire time because I was so upset. I was shouting out to God, 'Why do I have to miss out on everything? Why is it always me?' At this point in time I couldn't find any reason to smile. Nothing anyone could say made me feel better. It was a vicious cycle.

The only thing that made me feel better at the time was seeing my boyfriend and just hugging him. I kept apologising to him because I was sick and because we couldn't hang out together. He said, 'It's not your fault that you are sick. Don't apologise. These things happen. Just try to get better.' He had my best interests at heart; he was so supportive.

I wrote the above paragraph when I had had the virus for 12 days, thinking it would soon be over. Well, it lasted nearly two whole months! That was not normal. They felt like the longest two months of my life. It didn't feel like I was getting any better, but that each day I was only getting worse. I had no strength in me to keep fighting. My Christmas holidays were pretty much spent entirely in bed. All my plans for the break, such as cooking meals with Mum and catching up with friends, had to be cancelled. None of it happened. I didn't have the energy to meet up with friends even for a few hours.

To make matters worse, during this time my boyfriend and I broke up owing to differences in plans for our futures. It was not the best timing. I was devastated emotionally, and I couldn't function physically. But I had to continue moving forward and looking after my body. I had to stay strong for myself. I had been 'over' having this virus after two weeks, let alone two months. I was also experiencing really bad migraines, so I had a CT scan done to rule out anything serious. They found a build-up of fluid in my ear. So I had to see two specialists that month. The first one was a gastroenterologist, and the second an ENT specialist.

At the gastroenterologist consultation I had to wait an hour to see the specialist. Honestly, the number of times I have waited for doctors in waiting rooms is endless, but it has taught me how to be patient. When I finally saw her, I informed her of the duration of the virus, and she seemed very concerned. She booked me in for an endoscopy and a colonoscopy the following week. So, before I knew it, I was about to have two more medical procedures done. I had actually made it my New Year's resolution to *not* be in hospital again that year, yet here I was once again booking myself into a medical facility, albeit this time only a day surgery. I was very frustrated at this point, and at times felt like giving up. But I knew that by getting this endoscopy and colonoscopy done, I would be closer to solving my problem.

Before I knew it, the day had arrived. I had done everything to prepare for it. This involved drinking a litre of some strange solution (to clean my insides out) the night before, and fasting for 24 hours before the procedure. The solution didn't taste too bad, but it was the fasting that I couldn't handle. By the time the day of the procedure came around I was so hungry and weak that I felt like I was going to pass out.

I arrived at the hospital with Mum at 2:30pm for my appointment with the ENT specialist. Seeing as both of the appointments were in the same hospital, I was praying the whole way there that we would get in really quickly and we wouldn't have to wait around for long. As Mum and I entered the waiting room, I noticed it was completely empty. We were the only ones there. I filled out the required paperwork and within five minutes I was called in.

As I entered the specialist's office I could see lots of medical tools sitting in their assigned places, a screen above, and a bed to the right of it. He looked at my scans and told us that there was nothing to worry about. The fluid in my ear had been picked on an earlier scan and completely forgotten about. After looking in my ear he then grabbed a spray and sprayed inside both of my nostrils. He told me it was a local anaesthetic, so he could have a look up there. He walked outside to get something. I turned to Mum with a worried look and said, 'I think he wants to put something up my nose.'

When he came back in he was holding a 30-centimetre flexible tube with a light at the end of it. He said that he wanted me to tilt my head back so he could look inside my nostrils. I started freaking out, and turned my head away from him. He reassured me that two-year-olds had this done, and I wouldn't feel a thing. I kept looking at the length of it. I thought he wanted to put the tube up one nostril and out the other one, but thankfully I was wrong. He told me it was now numb inside my nose, and that it would only be slightly uncomfortable. After about five minutes of plucking up courage, I finally gave in and let him put the tube up. I had overreacted; it wasn't that bad, only a little uncomfortable, and thankfully he only used about ten centimetres of the tube. I was very glad when it was all over. He could find nothing wrong, and told me only to come back and see him if my headaches came back or if anything out-of-the-ordinary ensued. So that was the first test checked off my list. There was nothing to worry about. I felt relieved.

Next it was time to check in with the endoscopy unit. I had all of my admission papers ready to go. I weighed myself and found out I had now lost another three kilos. So in the entire two months I had this virus I lost a total of eight kilos. It was scary. The nurse gave me a gown, slippers and a hat to change into. I said goodbye to Mum and was ushered into a room, where I found a girl watching TV. I could have completely ignored her and just watched TV too, but my chaplaincy skills kicked in. I introduced myself and we started getting to know each other. She was so friendly and open with me that I felt like I had known her for ages. When she eventually was called to go into theatre we wished each other all the best.

As soon as she disappeared behind the theatre doors, I knew it would be my turn next. It was a production line – like before you start off on a roller-coaster ride and are still indoors, where it's all dark and the cars are all lined up ready to go. The car in front of you leaves, and the doors close behind it. Your car starts to pull up, and you know that you are next. That was how it felt. Her hospital bed had been wheeled into theatre before me, and I knew as soon as she was 'done', I would be next.

Lying on the bed alone with my thoughts, I started to get frightened. Opposition started to come at me. Thoughts like 'You're going to feel the whole thing' and 'You couldn't even last two months without being back in hospital'. Also, the thought of the cannula scared me, and I was preparing myself for more than one attempt, as usual. As this fear started to creep in, I stopped it. I recognised it straight away and started to speak with authority, quoting Bible verses:

Do not fear, for I am with you…

Isaiah 41:10

and,

(His) perfect love drives out (all) of fear.

1 John 4:18

I kept repeating these words, speaking boldly, and they eventually calmed my nerves.

I was finally ready to be wheeled into theatre. As I entered the doors, it instantly felt cold and I could smell antiseptic everywhere. I saw a screen that was turned off hanging above me, and I guessed that was where the camera would be recording what they were seeing inside me. Then the worst part – the cannula had to be put in my arm. This I never looked forward to, but I knew it had to be done.

The nurse started tapping my right hand, looking for a vein. She seemed to find one. I felt every bit of that pain. I'm not exaggerating, it was the worst cannula insertion I have ever experienced. I started swearing, screaming and crying. I asked if it was a good vein and the nurse shook her head, and they had to take it out. Then, without asking, she inserted another cannula just next to it, and once again there was unbearable pain. I started screaming, crying and swearing once again. One of the nurses who could see I was in distress grabbed my other hand, like a mother would do, and this gave me a bit of comfort. Once again the cannula didn't work, so she had to pull that one out too. Then she finally asked me where the best place normally was, and I pointed to my right arm. Once again I cried and screamed, but this time it worked. The last thing I remember was wiping away my tears, and then I blacked out.

I remember slowly waking up in recovery and seeing nurses walking around bringing in new patients. I woke up feeling relieved, and cried a little, just thanking God that it was all over. As I looked around, I noticed that everyone else was asleep; they still hadn't woken up. I was the only one awake. Then I saw a familiar face, that of my doctor. She came over to me and told me that the procedure had gone well, and that they hadn't found anything wrong. Then she left.

I was still a bit zoned out and had wanted to ask her more questions, but it was too late. I had a follow-up consultation in a week's time, so was going to have to wait till then.

One of the nurses woke me up properly, and brought a wheelchair to my bedside so I could be taken out of the recovery room, and then they gave me something to eat. After fasting for more than 24 hours, I was starving. This was the best meal I had had in a long time. As I started to eat, I could see the bruises where they had put the two unsuccessful cannulas in. I was so bruised and sore at this point that I couldn't even open my hand and close it. But, other than that, I had no pain, and that was a great feeling. Seeing Mum's face after the procedure was reassuring. She looked so proud of me and she was so supportive. I changed back into my clothes, they removed the cannula from my arm, and I was released to go home.

After hearing that the specialists had found nothing, I was in two frames of mind about things. Either a miracle had happened and I had been completely healed, or more tests needed to be done to determine if there was something else going on. I really didn't know what to do. I was at a dead end with the results, and all I could do was wait another week until the next consultation.

Before I knew it, one week had passed, and I was sitting with the gastroenterologist in the same room as before. It just happened to be Valentine's Day. She said the same thing – that both tests had gone well, and that they couldn't find anything wrong with me. However, she told me that because I had had the virus for so long (70 days to be exact), it had caused an infection which had had stripped the inner lining of my stomach. As a result I was having issues with digestion.

Basically, as I understood it, there are enzymes in your body which aid the digestion of your food. These enzymes in my stomach were not breaking down lactose and gluten as they should, so I was told that I would have to eliminate all lactose and gluten from my diet. She also told me not to eat processed foods. I was given a long list of things I was not allowed to eat. It seemed endless. I started to question exactly what was left that I *could* eat.

This diet was not easy at first, and cutting those foods out of my life was a struggle. I had always loved my dairy products, and was the biggest chocoholic ever. So to say goodbye to chocolate and sweets was a really big struggle for me. But the pain in my stomach after I ate those foods was much worse. So that helped me stay away from unhealthy foods.

I eventually learnt to enjoy gluten-free, lactose-free and non-processed foods. I really appreciated being able to buy those specialist foods that cater for specific dietary requirements. I never thought I would be a person who checked the ingredients on the back of food packets or who brought her own food to parties or events. Birthday parties were especially hard, as I missed out on all the delicious treats and birthday cake.

My doctor had told me that these dietary requirements would either resolve themselves in three months, or otherwise would need to be adhered to my whole life. I was praying and hoping it would only be three months. After three months had passed, every now and then I tried one of my foods on the 'forbidden' list, but it still resulted in uncomfortable stomach pains. But I still hadn't lost hope. I decided that even if things went back to normal and my stomach was able to handle gluten and lactose again, I wouldn't go back to my old ways. After a few weeks of changing my diet I had begun to feel really fit and healthy. I was really enjoying my new self. If I hadn't branched out of my comfort zone, I would never have known how good gluten-free and lactose-free products tasted, or how healthier I felt on them.

During this whole experience I lost 10 kilograms, and my confidence and body-image positivity grew. I felt really great for the first time in a while. Everyone said I had a glow about me and I looked different. My plan had been to lose weight by working out; this had been a very fast way to reach that goal.

There are two ways you can react to change – either you can accept it and adapt to it, or you can groan and complain about it. At first, I admit, I complained about the change in my diet. It was unfair. But then I grew to accept it and adapt to it, which was the better alternative because in the end it made me feel very positive and healthy. I can tell you that a miracle happened, and this intolerance lasted only for six months. It didn't persist indefinitely, like the doctor said it might. I was very happy with the result.

LET'S SAY A PRAYER

Lord, I pray that when I get bad news from the doctor, or when some other storm is raging in my life, I will trust in you. Help me to know that you are in control, and that you are a faithful God. Lord, there might be instant healing or it might take a long time, but either way I pray that I will be patient and stay faithful. I believe in miracles. I believe that you are a healing God, and that you will heal me. *All* things are possible with you. Help me to keep on living without letting this storm restrict me, and help me to stay positive and keep hoping in you. I ask for this in Jesus' name. Amen.

CHAPTER REVIEW

- Nothing is impossible with God.
- Don't let sickness become your identity.
- Sometimes a setback is a setup for something greater.
- It is all about your attitude – how you react to the situation.
- Miracles *do* happen.
- God *is* in control.
- *There is a God.*

Chapter 14
LIFE LEECHES

'Heaven and earth will pass away, but my words will never pass away...'

Matthew 24:35

My troubles continued after the nerve healing in my leg. Everything was a mess. I had the gastro virus for 70 days. I was living with emotional pain after a really hard relationship break-up. I felt like I had no purpose in life, and that I had lost my identity. However, at this stage a friend of mine helped me to move forward by opening my eyes to something that I was utterly unaware of.

One night when I was praying, God prompted me to ask this friend for advice and prayer support. When I had sought her help in the past, she had been always been straightforward and confronting (rather than gentle and loving) in her response. I now had reached the point where I needed her honest intervention once again, whether it be delivered gently or not.

So I approached this friend and opened up about having an identity crisis, and how I felt I had lost my way. I complained about all the suffering that kept coming my way. She immediately replied, 'All of this illness and pain is not normal.' I agreed. Then she said something *very* confronting: 'Do you think that part of you subconsciously hangs on to being unwell as a means of getting attention?' Woah! That shocked me to the core, and made me really question myself. I told her that I would need to go away and think about it, pray about it and search deep within myself to find the answer. I had never had this suggested to me before. We ended with a prayer and I went home.

That whole week I prayed very hard, searching deeply with God, and questioning the reason why I was always sick. What was revealed to me was equally as shocking – I could barely believe what I was hearing. God showed me that, without realising it, illness had in fact *become my identity*. Because I had grown up knowing endless sicknesses and problems, I had developed an invalid consciousness, to the extent that when I *didn't* feel unwell then I didn't feel normal. I felt empty without my sickness and pain. It wasn't attention-seeking at all; it was simply that I knew no other way of living. It *was* an identity-crisis. I couldn't believe that all of this had happened in my life without my being aware of it, and that I had been so deceived. Now I finally knew the reason I was always sick – because I was opening the door to sickness and letting it restrict me.

There had been times when my mind would battle with me, part of me wanting to be well and another part expecting myself to be ill. I was being double-minded without even realising it. Part of me felt comfortable being sick, and the other stronger part didn't want to live with the restrictions of sickness. However, once sickness struck, I wanted it cured as quickly as possible. I was letting sickness rule and reign in my life. Once I figured this out, it was a huge revelation for me. I realised that this way of thinking needed to be immediately stopped. But I knew it wouldn't be easy. How many times have you promised God that you would stop some unhelpful habit, yet never had the strength to actually change? I think we have all suffered from this problem.

I realised that, without my knowing it, sickness and pain had had such a hold over my life. Now, enough was enough! It was time to end it once and for all.

So that very day I made a commitment to God. I told Him that every morning when I woke up I would say out loud, 'I shut the door to all pain and sickness. It will no longer reign in my life. My identity is found in you, God. In your name I command all future sickness to be gone, and I shut the door right now to any pain. I give you the key, God, and I ask that you throw it into the deepest ocean so that that door can never be reopened.'

I started to speak in faith and authority over my body any time a little headache or stomach-ache started coming on, and almost instantly the pain would disappear. I prayerfully shut the door to all pain and illness, and refused to allow it to stop me from living life to the full. Pain would no longer stop me from being the person God had created me to be, nor to limit me in doing the will of God in my life.

As soon as pain or suffering presented itself, I would usually lie down and dwell on it. If you, dear reader, are going through any sort of pain right now, don't dwell on it, but rather give it to God. Remember that we serve a mighty God, one who is far greater than our pain. He is a healing God. Jesus died not only to take away our sins and shame and sorrows, but also our sicknesses, both physical, emotional and mental. Learn to speak in authority over your pain or sickness, and you will be amazed at what God will do. Command the sickness and pain to be gone in Jesus' name. Get out of your bed and start living again. There is power in prayer. There is power in the name of Jesus. In the name of Jesus, chains break. In the name of Jesus, demons flee. In the name of Jesus, love is restored. In the name of Jesus, healing takes place. *Praise Him!*

FEAR OF THE FUTURE

When you receive a negative report from your doctor, don't let it consume you. In situations like this, I would always let fear take hold of me. My hope would disappear and fear would take over. Fear is like a leech that will not let go of you, if you allow it to.

I remember one year experiencing really severe pains in my groin area. This pain started cropping up monthly, but then became a weekly occurrence – and eventually a daily one. Once it was so uncomfortable that I nearly took myself off to the hospital, thinking it might be appendicitis. But thankfully it wasn't. At the time I was a volunteer at the hospital once a week, so I decided to book in for an ultrasound during my lunch break. The radiographer conducting the ultrasound told me, 'Everything looks good.' This made me feel a huge sense of relief. But when I received the official results back a few days later, I was shocked to read that they had found 17 cysts on my right ovary.

My doctor told me that they could surgically remove the cysts by popping them, but there was a high likelihood of them returning. They apparently were not large enough to be operated on, and simply needed to be monitored. The reason I had been in pain was because one of the cysts had burst.

My doctor told me that it would take a whole month for it to pass through my system, and I remember it being a very painful time. I couldn't do anything more than go to work and then head straight back to bed. It was a very restricting time. But once the month had passed, I went back to normal again very quickly.

My doctor warned me that, as a result of these cysts, I might experience issues with having children later on. He warned that it could possibly lead to miscarriages along the way. When you hear news like that, you start to fear for the future. I want to be a mother one day, to have my own family. Hearing this created doubts in me, and was very upsetting at the time. But then I remembered someone else who had experienced the same condition, and who now was happily married with three children. And, more importantly, I remembered that God is bigger than anything I might have to face. And my heart was at peace once again. What I have learnt from this is that a setback can sometimes be a setup for something greater. So never doubt what God is doing in your life. He has a plan.

Since that appointment I have been monitoring my cysts, and all 17 of them have completely disappeared. What an amazing miracle. God is good. Never doubt what God can do in your life. *Nothing is impossible with Him.* Maybe your doctor has told you some bad news. All I can say is, trust God. He is in control of your life. Whatever the doctor says is *not* the final outcome. God can change any situation.

Sometimes we have to ride out the storm, like I had to endure a whole month of pain – but once it was over, that was it. At other times God will heal us after an extended period of prayer, as I experienced with my hip pain leaving a day after being prayed for. Yet at other times God will calm the storm instantly. I witnessed this whilst on a mission trip to the Philippines. I saw somebody's eyesight instantly restored, an enlarged heart instantly reduced back to its normal size, and crippled people instantly cured and walking again. Nothing is impossible with God. Have faith in Him. Sometimes God will calm the heart rather than the storm. This is a very important lesson too.

Being in the Philippines was quite confronting. There you cannot depend on anyone except God. You are there to do His work, to be His vessel, and when He opens doors and opportunities you obey in faith, knowing that He is by your side, and that He will give you the right words to say, the right people to minister to, and precisely the right timing for everything. I want to reassure you that there *is* a God and there *are* such things as miracles. I know this because I have witnessed them personally many times.

SCARS ARE BEAUTIFUL

Owing to the many surgeries that I've had, I've been left with many scars. At first they embarrassed me. I would try to conceal them so that nobody would see them. It took me a while to realise that scars are actually beautiful, that they tell a story of victory in having overcome many storms. Scars do fade in time, but they will always be a reminder of how you overcame a painful thing in your life.

Someone else who had scars was Jesus. When He died on the cross, there were many wounds on his body – on His back from the flogging, in His side from the spear, on his Head from the crown of thorns and on His hands and feet from the nails. After Jesus was resurrected, his wounds were seen as scars. These scars were evidence of His suffering, and of the freedom He won for us on the day of His crucifixion. They will forever be there as marks of His love for us.

We too have wounds, whether they be physical, emotional or mental. These wounds will be open and painful until we ask God for healing. This might first require us to forgive someone for wounding us. Or we might first need to let go of an emotional loss, or give over the pain of the remembrance of something unpleasant, for example a surgery. God can heal our wounds so that all we are left with are scars that no longer hurt us. And He will make our scars beautiful in time.

Hope in the Storms

LET'S SAY A PRAYER

Lord, I pray that I will never let fear, harsh words or bad experiences be a leech in my life. I pray that I will not allow pain of any kind to stop me from living my life victoriously. I pray that I will use my scars to encourage others to find healing in You. I pray that my scars will serve as a reminder of my victory over every storm. I pray this in Jesus' name. Amen

CHAPTER REVIEW
- Fear can be a leech if you let it.
- Don't let pain stop you from living your life.
- God is greater than your pain.
- God is a healing God.
- There is power in prayer.
- God wants to work through you.
- God can change your wounds into scars.
- Scars can be beautiful.

Chapter 15
FINDING JOY IN THE NEGATIVES

Consider it pure joy, my brothers and sisters, whenever you face trials of many kinds, because you know that the testing of your faith produces perseverance.
                                         James 1:2–3

After my boyfriend and I broke up, I felt that nothing in my life was going right. I felt alone, with nothing new or exciting to look forward to. I was focusing on the break-up so much that I was becoming very depressed. At the same time I was battling the gastro virus, as well as being forced to change my diet. So there were a many things going on in my life at the same time. I needed to snap out of my negative way of thinking, so I decided to look for a hobby or find something else to focus on. I considered joining a local sports club or a social group, but after looking online I didn't find myself drawn to anything on offer.

What I did find was an amateur theatrical society which was only about 15 minutes' drive from my home. As I perused their website, I read that the following week they were having auditions for the comedy production *The Perfect Wedding*. I questioned myself, 'Am I ready for this, if I end up being cast in a role?' At this point in my life I simply wanted something to change for the better. I just wanted to be busy. One part of me was afraid of auditioning for a role – because I knew that it would require a huge commitment, and also because I knew that my health was not something I could rely on. The other part of me needed to be busy and focused on something else. So, after much deliberation, I decided to go ahead and see what transpired.

The audition was to take place on Valentine's Day, which was hard for me. Instead of being out with my boyfriend (we had recently broken up), I would now be auditioning for the role of the bride in the production, and I wasn't sure that I would either get it or succeed at it if I did. Also, that same morning, my specialist had told me that I was gluten- and lactose-intolerant. So the day was already a struggle for me, long before the audition began. I was fairly nervous, and had asked a friend to tag along for support.

Upon arrival at the theatre my fears immediately vanished, and I was filled with excitement at meeting new people. We had to do a group audition, and this took me into my comfort zone. Then the time came, I was called up onto the stage with two guys, and I read my script with confidence. I didn't shake or panic once. I felt like I was meant to be there, and that nothing else mattered. After it was over I went back to my seat feeling very confident, and not bothered if I got the role or not. I was just so proud that I had been able to perform on stage in front of people that I didn't know.

Two days later I received an email from the director saying that she was considering me for the role. My heart leapt with excitement – but I was also filled with fear. What if I couldn't learn my lines properly? What if I was the only new person there? What if I became ill during the show? One of the questions the director asked me was, 'Can you learn lines quickly?' This question scared me a little because I realised that if I said 'no', then she would possibly not consider me. I now knew that there would be huge pressure to learn lines. So, knowing my capacity for learning song lyrics quickly, I replied that I was an average learner.

The next day I received an email saying that I had been cast in the role of Rachel, the bride. I was so excited that I was over the moon. This was something new to me; I had performed in plays at my church, but nothing on this scale – this production involved 16 performances over 4 weeks, in front of an audience of about one hundred and fifty people.

Even though this was outside my comfort zone and very confronting, I found joy in the experience. I learnt so many new skills, as well as many new things about myself. I was able to spend many interesting hours with the crew, both at the rehearsals and the actual performances. Seeing as it was a small group, we bonded extremely well. Throughout the entire time I incurred only two injuries and had one major migraine, and despite them still managed to push through. As I told the others, 'The show must go on.'

Because I was now focusing all of my time, energy and passion on something that I was growing to love, I started forgetting about my break-up, my singleness and how alone and depressed I was. I would practise my lines every night, so by the time rehearsals started I had learnt nearly all of them. Everyone, especially the director, was very impressed. After each of the performances I was so encouraged by the positive feedback I received from people in the audience that I had never met before.

Some of them were amazed that this was my first performance. They kept telling me that I should continue with my acting, seeing as I had such talent for it. This made me feel really proud of myself. During one rehearsal there were some professional actors observing, and one of the ladies came up to me and told me that I had a very strong presence on stage, and encouraged me to continue auditioning for other productions once this one was over. So I did!

If you are going through something difficult in your life, then I encourage you to focus your time, energy and passion elsewhere. Either do something new (and cross it off your bucket list), or go back to something that you loved doing in the past. All in all, invest your time in something that you find joy in. It might take time to adjust to it, but keep reminding yourself that each new day brings you one step closer to achieving your goal. Remember that in any situation you can always find positives. You may need a magnifying glass to find them, but they are always there.

Find joy in something new – work towards it and focus all your time, energy and passion in it. You will find this so rewarding. If you enjoy encouraging others, maybe you could spend time with the elderly. If you love children, maybe you could try babysitting. If you love travelling, then book a flight to a great holiday destination. You may have a long list of things you wish to achieve. Start now. What is stopping you?

After the play was over, I felt unstoppable. I decided that this was my year to be independent, to cross things off my bucket list. So I booked a trip with my best friend to a place where there was snow, and found so much joy in being in it for the first time in my life. For that whole week my mind was focused on simply enjoying the time there, and I didn't once think about my work or health. By the end of the trip I had experienced so many new things, such as skiing, building a snowman, having snowball fights and 'doing a snow angel'. Now that I have crossed those items off, I'm ready for the next one.

By the end of the week it had dawned on me that if I had had a boyfriend at the time, then I probably wouldn't have taken the trip and had those wonderful new experiences. God's timing is perfect. He knows when you are ready for a new relationship (or marriage, or children). You need to learn to trust Him.

AN UNEXPECTED LOVE STORY

As you will have gathered from what you have already read, my love-life has been a difficult journey. I have been hurt by many guys in my past, and many of my relationships haven't worked out. But during the performance of *The Perfect Wedding*, the person who played my fiancé started messaging me quite a bit, and we slowly started getting to know each other, and eventually started dating.

Before I met Dan I looked for guys everywhere because I was aware that I was getting older. God reassured me, 'Stop looking to the left and the right. I will bring him to you.' So when God brought Dan to me, I trusted Him with this relationship right from the beginning.

It was not love at first sight. When we first met at the auditions, I never even felt a spark. Neither did he. I was too uptight at the time, and he seemed a little bit immature to me then. The spark developed later on.

In the play Dan was my fiancé, and we had to share many on-stage kisses, which at the time was quite confronting for me, being my first-ever show. Dan was not the type of guy

I would normally have gone for. Part of me liked him, and another part of me was in denial of those feelings. However, as I got to know him I started seeing his amazingly genuine and beautiful heart.

The first time I saw his caring side was during one of the performances. It was a Wednesday night and I was about to leave for the theatre when, out of nowhere, a migraine hit me. I'd had migraines my whole life, and this was a pretty severe one. I had to lie down for about twenty minutes in a dark room to let it pass. I messaged everyone in the show and they were all so supportive. I couldn't drive because my head was spinning, so my dad dropped me off at the theatre and Dan offered to drive me back home after the show.

Sitting in the dressing room, I was pale, my head was spinning and I could barely walk. I had never before experienced these symptoms after a migraine. Normally I experience a lingering headache, but never dizziness – so this had me worried. My director came in and asked me if I was able to proceed with the show. I told her that I first needed to rest a while, but that I would be okay. Luckily for me there was a bed on the set for one of the first scenes, so I was able to lie down while the rest of the cast did their usual warm-ups.

During this particular Wednesday performance the stage direction had to be changed to accommodate my health needs, and the stage manager had to hold me up before I made my first entrance. Then, instead of standing up by myself during the play, Dan had to hold me up. He was so supportive, as were the rest of the cast and crew. The lady who played my mother also helped me up when she was on stage. We made it all look like it was part of the show. Nobody even knew. Even backstage during intermission I had to rest – and Dan was by my side. It was then that I started to see a brand-new side to him. After the performance finished Dan drove me home, walked me to my door and made sure I got in safely.

It wasn't until after the production *The Perfect Wedding* finished that Dan and I started messaging and hanging out with each other more frequently. We didn't call these times spent together 'dates'. We rather referred to them as 'friendly hangouts'!

Two months later, while we were messaging each other, a conversation arose about why we were both still single. It was then that Dan brought up the idea of us officially going out on a date. I initially turned him down because I still wasn't sure about him. But he managed to convince me to try just one date to see how it would go.

Our first date was very relaxed, and by the end of it we couldn't deny the feelings that we were starting to have for each other. So we decided to continue seeing each other and going on other dates. Normally I would ask other people for their opinions on a guy I was dating, but this time I went into the relationship completely by myself. I wanted to do this alone, with nobody else's influence or perspective. The only other person I included in this relationship was God, and when I had prayed about it He responded by saying, 'Trust me. I have this.' Even to this day I trust God with this relationship, and I thank Him for bringing Dan into my life in such an unexpected way.

Once I was comfortable with Dan and realised that it was a serious relationship, I informed my parents and friends. Even though it was very different to my usual relationships, they supported me in it, which meant a lot. Even though we both had very different backgrounds, we respected each other's values.

We really did bring out the best in each other. He helped me to learn how to 'go with the flow' and live in the present rather than stress about the future.

By the time we reached our first anniversary, I knew that this relationship would last. Prior to this, the longest I had been in a relationship was just under six months. His longest relationship had lasted only three months. So, for both of us, this was our first serious relationship. He proposed to me after one and a half years of being together, and we married and bought our first home. I now look back on my past relationships and I am so thankful that God closed those doors – because if He hadn't then I would never have met this incredible guy.

Marriage is a wonderful place to learn about living as a Christian, because nobody is perfect. I am still learning, and will continue to do so all my life. God is teaching me to be quick to forgive and to love unconditionally. I am also learning not to judge others, but rather to look beyond their faults; to love them for who they are, and to support them in their struggles and celebrate with them in their victories. It is a journey that my husband and I are taking together.

LET'S SAY A PRAYER

Lord, I pray that when you close certain doors in my life and open others that I will trust you. Lord, you know my future, and you are writing my love story. Even when things don't go my way, Lord, help me to believe that you are still in control. You know what is best for my life. Help me to find joy in all that I face. Help me to find the positives in all situations. I ask this in your name, Jesus. Amen.

CHAPTER REVIEW

- Put your trust in God.
- Find something that you love doing and focus on it.
- Ask God to help you find joy, even in hardships.
- Look for the positives in every situation.
- Keep persevering, even when doors close.
- Nobody is perfect.

Chapter 16
INCURABLE DOES NOT MEAN FINAL

> This is the confidence we have in approaching God: that if we ask anything according to his will, he hears us.
>
> 1 John 5:14

After my return from the trip to the snow I suffered for about two weeks from a really bad headache and dizziness. First of all I tried exercising, as I thought it might be the result of a physical injury. When this made no difference, my doctor diagnosed a sinus infection, and prescribed various medications, none of which worked. Because the pain was concentrated in the middle of my forehead, she booked me in for an MRI of the frontal lobe of my brain. It was then that she joked with me that every time she saw me she felt she might have a panic attack because I never seemed to have anything normal about my diagnoses. She told me to stop getting sick; I told her I wasn't doing it on purpose.

I was very anxious in the week leading up to the scan. My headache kept steadily worsening, until my head felt like it was going to explode. At that point I just wanted them to find out what was wrong.

Eventually it was time for the scan. I remember sitting at

the medical centre with my mum. This felt like *déjà vu;* like I was reliving the process of my tumour discovery. I had only waited about five minutes when a gentleman called my name. I followed him to the scanning room, and after a few questions I was placed in the MRI machine. As I lay there I couldn't help but feel a little bit afraid. I was in the very same machine where I had had the initial tumour diagnosis. I was alone with my thoughts – never a good place to be at a time like this. There was some music being played through the headphones, so I tried to focus on the sound and not the voices in my head. It seemed to work because I fell asleep to the music.

When it was over I was told I would receive my scans in a day or two, and that my results would be sent to my doctor. As you can imagine, those few days were so nerve-racking for me. I kept thinking of the worst-case scenario. When I finally received my scans back, I was relieved to find they were all clear. Nothing abnormal had been found. I was relieved that I didn't have a tumour or anything else that was serious. But I still wanted to know what was causing these symptoms.

The next day I went back to see my doctor. She said that she was glad the scans had come back clear, but she was still really concerned about me. She mentioned she thought I might be suffering from something called Meniere's disease. It seemed that she had been doing quite a bit of researching and thinking about this. She firmly believed that I had this condition, and all of my symptoms lined up with this diagnosis. She told me that it wasn't a very common condition, especially for a person of my age. Meniere's disease is an inner-ear disorder that causes progressive deafness and attacks of tinnitus and vertigo. That would account for the build-up of fluid that my ENT specialist had found in my inner ear. Also, I had had intermittent ringing in my ears (tinnitus) over the years, but thought it was normal.

The next step was to get a hearing test administered, as this condition usually presents with fullness in the ears and some degree of hearing loss owing to the pressure build-up in the inner ear.

The week before my hearing test was due, I went on a trip to Melbourne with my colleagues. I had never been there before, so it was great to once again cross something off my bucket list. Whilst there we did a huge amount of shopping and eating, and I became aware that all the meals I had there were very unhealthy. Throughout the trip I experienced a constant headache and dizziness. So much so that it was sometimes hard to focus. When the girls went out for a walk I had to stay behind at the hotel because of a debilitating headache. Once again I felt like I was missing out on things.

The day after our return I had an appointment with the audiologist. Before she started any tests she asked me many questions in order to get an idea of what I was experiencing. After listening to what I had to say, she came to the same initial conclusion as my doctor – that I had Meniere's disease. She also strongly believed that my migraines were indicative of this condition.

Then came the time for the hearing test. The first thing she did was to place an apparatus in my ear. This played increasing volumes of sound, until it got to the stage that there was so much pressure in my ear that it felt like it was going to explode. She then repeated this on the other ear. These results all came back clear – this indicated that my outer-ear condition was normal.

The next test was on my inner ear, and was a reaction test.

This time she played me various sounds at different volumes, through headphones. I had to press a button every time I heard a sound. The results showed that I had relatively good overall hearing, but that I was not too clear with high pitches or loud sounds.

The last test was a hearing-and-reflecting test (at least this is what I called it). I had words spoken to me through headphones at varying volumes, and I had to repeat them out loud. Once again, my responses were good; once again, nothing significant was found. At this stage she told me that because at the time I hadn't been having an episode, and because there was no current pressure build-up in my ears, the tests couldn't really confirm anything. She said that the next time I experienced symptoms (and was in the area) I could ring them up and have the test repeated free of charge, and that I would be prioritised over everyone else.

The day after the hearing test I went back to see my doctor, who said that she strongly believed that I definitely *was* suffering from Meniere's disease, but that she wanted me to see my ENT specialist for confirmation. So the following week I went to see him. He said that he *didn't* think I had Meniere's disease, because apparently headaches are not one of the symptoms of this condition. He instead believed I was suffering from vestibular migraines. I had always experienced migraines; in fact, they were very common in my family. So it did make some sense to me that this could be a possibility.

About a week later, whilst talking to someone at church, I suddenly began to have an episode. I was wearing sunglasses at the time, so the friend had no idea of what was happening. I calmly told her that I needed to leave, and started walking off. It started with mini aura spots appearing in my field of vision, and before I knew it my entire vision was clouded and I couldn't see. Next everything started to spin, and I struggled to remain standing. Then my ear began to fill up with so much pressure that I thought it was going to explode. Lastly, I felt shortness of breath, and couldn't speak.

By this stage I had fully accepted my diagnosis of Meniere's disease, and possibly also vestibular migraines. I now found myself in bed sick most of the time. I became very miserable and frustrated. Once again I thought, 'Why me?' This was the first time in my life that I felt truly defeated. This affected my personal relationships and working life dramatically. I couldn't focus at work, and I had to cancel many of my social arrangements because I felt so depressed and sick.

I had a pretty severe attack one time at work. This happened just a few weeks after I had been diagnosed with Meniere's disease. I was assisting my boss with emails, when all of a sudden I couldn't maintain my balance. I was sitting down in front of my computer and I couldn't get my bearings. I simply couldn't work out where I was at the time. I felt like I was floating in the air with my legs above me. I couldn't focus on one spot. It was the weirdest feeling I had ever experienced.

I gripped my desk in disorientation and fear, and this seemed to help a little bit, despite everything spinning around me. I cried out to my boss and told him that something was very wrong. Slowly and carefully he walked me over to the couch so that I could lie down. It was a very scary experience. As a result of all the spinning I was experiencing, I started to feel nauseous. After it cleared up I lost my appetite and couldn't eat for a few days. It took me about a full week to recover completely.

After that episode I went back to see my ENT specialist,

who told me to get some more tests done in order to confirm that it was in fact Meniere's disease. So I went back to the audiologist for some more tests. The first was a hearing test – when I heard a sound, I had to press a button. For the second test I had to stare at a dot and follow it around the room with my eyes, left to right, up and down. It started off slowly and then gradually got faster, to the point where I couldn't follow it anymore because I couldn't concentrate. I struggled with this test because moving my eyes from left to right at a fast pace made me feel dizzy.

The third and final test was very uncomfortable. I had to wear a helmet-like device with large goggles which had a visor that could be opened or closed. I started feeling a bit claustrophobic even before the test began. The goggles tracked my eye movements and reactions to the various stimuli. The test involved blowing cold air into each ear for about a minute. This was not only very uncomfortable, but also brought on an attack of vertigo. My normal reaction when feeling dizzy is to close my eyes, but with this test I had to try to keep them open so that they could observe my eye movement. At the same time that I was experiencing vertigo, the audiologist was asking me random questions. Then she changed it to blowing hot air in my ears, and the same thing happened all over again. It took me a few hours to recuperate after the test, and I was so relieved when it was finally over.

About three weeks later I went back to my ENT specialist to get the results, and he said that my hearing was perfect. He told me that I could expect my hearing to fluctuate, and that driving could be an issue in the future because of the vertigo episodes. He also said that these episodes would come in waves, and that I would not be able to predict them.

After leaving his office I got into my car and started driving to work. This was the first time that after hearing bad health news that I was able to keep smiling and laughing. Up to this stage each time I had received a bad diagnosis I would spend that whole day reflecting negatively on it and being depressed. But this time I was able to smile and laugh – because I didn't believe that I had to live with this disease. I believed that I would receive healing. I knew that God had my life in the palm of His hand, and I trusted Him so much. I knew that He had always been faithful to me, and that He wouldn't stop now. I realised that it was all about one's *attitude* to hearing bad news. *That's* what mattered. *That's* what shaped the outcome.

At this stage I started doing my own research, and realised that in Melbourne I had been eating a lot of salty foods. This realisation, combined with my doctor's advice, started me on a brand-new salt-restricted diet of fresh fruits and vegetables – and in two days I noticed a dramatic change. In just over a month I finally experienced relief from the headaches and dizziness. I finally felt free and unrestricted.

DIAGNOSIS DOESN'T MEAN DEFINITE

The word 'diagnosis' is a pretty strong one. It feels like it's definite, like it's been set in concrete. It makes you think that you will be living with the condition for the rest of your life. Well, guess what – when you are diagnosed with something, it does *not* need to be permanent.

Our God is bigger and is stronger than that diagnosis. Our God is faithful. He is a healing God. Believe for a miracle to happen. Nothing is impossible or incurable with Him. God doesn't want to see us suffer. He doesn't want us to be restricted in life – He wants us to live in freedom so we can fulfil our mission in life, which is to share the Good News with others.

There is currently no cure for Meniere's disease, but one can find relief through various medications and a few risky surgeries. In my case, I believed a miracle would take place. I did not believe that I would ever become deaf. I did not believe that I would go on having vertigo attacks to the point of feeling paralysed. I did not believe that I would possibly have my driver's licence taken away from me. I believed I would be healed. And today I praise God that I no longer am medically diagnosed as having Meniere's disease. My condition has finally and conclusively been diagnosed as vestibular migraines, thanks to my neurologist. I had to wait nearly six months to see him, as well as having more tests done – but it was worth it; he is great.

I still sometimes have vertigo attacks when I eat too many sodium-rich foods, but that's not every day. During these episodes my family is so supportive and caring. They look after me until I am completely better. I'm so blessed to have these people in my life. I still can't enjoy the salty foods that I sometimes crave, nor can I drink alcohol or caffeine without feeling dizzy. I have definitely had to sacrifice a lot, but it is all worth it. I find suitable and tasty alternatives, and I make the best of each difficult situation.

ONE IN 1000

The next storm that I faced only happens to about 1 in a 1000 people. All throughout my life I have noticed that if I simply bump or knock myself, I bruise instantly and quite noticeably. Also, if I accidentally cut myself, I continue bleeding much longer than other people do. I didn't understand why all this was happening to me. I thought it was normal.

I had two years of having to get a spate of blood tests done in order to monitor my low blood-platelet levels. If you don't know what blood platelets are, here is a quick explanation. When you cut yourself, the blood platelets rush to that area and create a clot so that you don't bleed excessively. The normal number of blood platelets someone is supposed to have is between 150,000 to 400,000. My tests normally showed my levels to be around 140,000, which is just under the lowest level considered healthy. One such test result even came in at 102,000, which is very low. The cause for concern was that if I were to fall over and bump my head (from the vertigo), my brain would likely bleed badly.

My doctor referred me to a haematologist, who was really positive and said that my levels were manageable, which is what I wanted to hear. However, she wanted me to get three blood tests done to check for any immune deficiencies. This was just in the room next to her. As you can imagine, that was a horrific time for me. As usual, the nurse had trouble trying to locate my veins, which are always hard to find. The needle she was using was one they use on babies, because my veins are so thin. When she finally found a vein, she put the needle in, but it worked only for a short while and then the blood just stopped flowing. So she had to look for another vein.

She found a second vein; however, by the time she had inserted the needle, there was no blood flow at all. By this time nearly 30 minutes had passed, and I was in a lot of pain from being poked and bruised. Also, I was frustrated because this always happened to me.

I then started to feel really chilly; my teeth started chattering and my whole body began to shake. I also began to feel really weak and breathless. They gave me blankets to keep me warm and then called another nurse over to find the third vein. This time only a little bit of blood came out. By this time they had only taken enough blood for two-thirds of the tests, but they decided that was enough. Then, after a few minutes of lying down and resting, I was finally able to stand up by myself and drive home. After a month of waiting for the results, they came back as normal, showing that my blood-platelets count had lifted to 140,000. But this is apparently something that I will have to have monitored for my entire life.

Maybe you are in a situation that feels unchangeable, or maybe your doctor has given you some really bad news. All I can say is this – believe God's promises in the Bible and expect a miracle to happen. Keep praying – because prayer is powerful. Prayer might not change the situation instantly, but it can still be used as a source of strength in hard times. Stay positive and find joy in the little things. Count every day as a blessing to be alive. Don't take any one of them for granted.

LET'S SAY A PRAYER

Lord, I pray that as I journey through this storm I will stay positive, and that my focus will be on finishing the race. I pray that my faith will increase, and that I will remain hopeful and thankful in everything. I pray that I will cast all of my anxiety and worry on you, because I know that you care about me. I pray that I will not let pain dictate my life. Help me not to surrender to it. I pray all of this in Jesus' name. Amen.

CHAPTER REVIEW

- A diagnosis does not mean that your situation will be permanent.
- Our God is a healing God.
- Always stay positive during your storms.
- God has set an end-date to your problems.
- Nothing is impossible or incurable with Him.
- Do not let pain be the dictator of your life.

Chapter 17
ANCHORED HOPE

> Now faith is confidence in what we hope for and assurance about what we do not see.
> Hebrews 11:1

The difference between hope and faith is this: faith believes and speaks out what it knows is going to happen, whereas hope prepares the mind to be strong, bold and courageous during stormy seasons in our lives. Faith claims and commands what is about to happen sometime soon. Hope expects and believes for better things to happen in the future. These two go hand in hand.

In Hebrews 6:19 it says that hope is an anchor for one's soul. We can have confidence and peace in the hope that we feel. Imagine a ship being tossed around by gigantic waves. The only way to stop the ship being driven off course is by dropping anchor. The role of an anchor in heavy weather is to stabilise the ship. Without it, the ship would be forced to submit to the waves and directed off course, which potentially could end with it crashing into something and sinking.

When you are in the middle of a storm and when doubts start threatening your faith, what is your anchor? Who or what is holding you firmly in place? Your faith may *feel* weak, but if it is anchored in the promises of God's word, He will safely hold you. When you feel the stress of the storm, that is when you must learn to trust the strength of the anchor. Dropping anchor means standing firm on God's word, which is a sure rock. *The safest thing you can do in a storm is to drop anchor and be still.*

Matthew 7 tells the story of two builders. The first one built his house on the sand, and when the flood came in it destroyed that house. The second one built his house on the rock, and when that flood came against it, it remained standing. The only difference between those two houses was their foundations. We need to build our lives on Jesus, the only sure and unshakeable Rock. We need to make the Word of God our foundation in life if we wish to remain strong and intact throughout the storms that come against us.

Think of a tree that has existed for over 100 years. It would be much harder to pull up the roots of that tree than to do so to a tree that had only recently been planted. That century-old tree would over time have grounded itself deeply into the soil. No storm or flood would easily be able to uproot or move it. No wind would be able to blow it away. Likewise, we need to ground ourselves so deeply in Jesus Christ that nothing and no one will be able to shake us. Root yourself in the faithfulness of God.

Should we only turn to and hope in God when life becomes a struggle and everything seems hopeless? The answer is NO. Our hope should *always* be in God, through the good seasons too. Hope is there as an anchor in all seasons.

When you need hope, you can't just ask for it and expect to receive it instantly. Hope is usually something that needs to be built up throughout one's life. It is built by spending time with God, getting to know who He is, and learning to trust Him and be dependent on Him. Others may help you and influence you, but true hope is found in God alone, and needs to be built up over time.

EVERYDAY HOPE VERSUS BIBLICAL HOPE

In our day-to-day conversations the word 'hope' is used widely and often. 'I hope it is sunny today.' 'I hope I pass my test.' 'I hope I find my wallet.' This type of hope has uncertain evidence in it. It is saying that we don't know what is going to happen in the end, but we wish that it will end in our advantage.

Biblical hope is very different to wishful thinking, and there is no unreliability about it. Biblical hope is faith in the future tense. Putting your hope in God doesn't mean 'fingers crossed'. It is having expectancy for your desire, asked for in prayer, to occur. It is having expectancy for that prayer to be answered. It believes for great things to happen. It means that every time you pray in line with the promises in God's word, you have hope and assurance that your prayers will be answered by your promise-keeping God.

Whenever I went through a storm in my life, I put my hope in God, knowing that He would get me through it. I even put my hope in God for healing – because salvation includes healing, and there is nothing impossible with Him.

When we put our hope in the Lord, there is no need to worry or be anxious about anything.

> **Even youths grow tired and weary, and young men stumble and fall; but those who hope in the Lord will renew their strength. They will soar on wings like**

eagles; they will run and not grow weary; they will walk and not be faint.

Isaiah 40:30-31

Putting hope in God becomes an energy boost to renew our strength because, whether we like it or not, tomorrow is never sure. When we place our hope in our everlasting God, we have a certainty and assurance that everything will be okay; rather than putting our energy in worrying or being anxious about things we can't change by ourselves, we should rather put our energy where it will make a difference.

Do you know where hope comes from? In Psalm 62:5 it says that hope comes from God alone. No one else can restore lost hope. Only God can. So not only do you put your hope *in* God, your hope *comes from* God. For this reason we can find rest *in* God. We have the sure knowledge that God will never let us down, nor will He ever abandon us.

And wherever there is full assurance of hope, is there faith too. It actually says in 1 Peter 3:15 that when asked why we have hope, we need always to be prepared to give a reason for that hope. Could you do that? What would you say? What makes you hopeful? Who do you put your hope in? Do you put your hope in God?

Here are some things that people put their hope in:

- an event that can change their life
- the weather
- locating something that was lost
- doctor's results
- sunrise on a new day

- the results of a pregnancy test
- the last turn on the poker machine
- the final number on the lottery
- family and friends
- the New Year
- the marks on an exam

All of the above are temporary things to hope for. God is eternal. Put your hope in Him, because He is the only one who knows your whole situation and He already has set an end date to it, if you will only believe it. Romans 8:28 tells us that all things work together for good for those that love Him and are called according to His purposes.

Jesus Christ is where we find our hope, where we can dance in the storms, where we can smile through the pain, where we can trust through the grief and where we can hope in the hopeless situations of our lives.

I would like to encourage all of you who are reading this book that there *is* hope. Hope comes in different forms for each and every one of us. I have written about my own personal experiences of hope. Your situations will be quite different. My intention, as I said at the beginning of this book, is for your hope to be restored. And if you have lost hope, that you find it again. Even when you are at the end of your rope, there is always someone you can hold on to. There is a God in whom you can put your hope. He is your Father in heaven, and He cares for you and will not let you down. He is not temporary; He is eternal. He is not dead; He is alive. He wants to have a relationship with you.

Through every storm that you go through, He is with you every step of the way and He will give you the strength you need to get through it. Storms are all temporary; they do not last forever. There is always a rainbow of hope waiting for you at the end.

I would like to end with a beautiful psalm which sums up who our God is...

> Praise the Lord!
> Let all that I am praise the Lord.
> I will praise the Lord as long as I live.
>   I will sing praises to my God with my dying breath.
> Don't put your confidence in powerful people;
>   there is no help for you there.
> When they breathe their last, they return to
>   the earth, and all their plans die with them.
> But joyful are those who have the God of Israel
>   as their helper, whose hope is in
>   the Lord their God.
> He made heaven and earth,
>   the sea, and everything in them.
>   He keeps every promise forever.
> He gives justice to the oppressed
>   and food to the hungry.
> The Lord frees the prisoners.
> The Lord opens the eyes of the blind.
> The Lord lifts up those who are weighed down.
>   The Lord loves the godly.
> The Lord protects the foreigners among us.
>   He cares for the orphans and widows,
>   but he frustrates the plans of the wicked.

Anchored Hope

The Lord will reign forever.
   He will be your God, O Jerusalem,
   throughout the generations.
Praise the Lord!
Psalm 146:1–10 (NLT)

About the Author

Chantal was brought up in a close-knit Christian home. Her faith journey started to take off when she was a teenager. She didn't let anything get in between her strong relationship with God. Her identity was in her faith in God.

But no matter where she went or what she did, Chantal always seemed to be in some sort of physical pain. There was always something wrong with her body, leading to innumerable scans, surgeries and hospitalisations. She felt as if she was always sick.

Most ailments she experienced were considered unusual for her age and gender. It never surprised her when doctors or surgeons couldn't solve her problems. Even when she had a cancer scare, the tumour the surgeon found was rare, especially for that particular location – he said that in all his 25 years in practice he had only seen one like that.

Other people grew up collecting stamps or coins; Chantal collected her own body scans – MRIs, ultrasounds and the like. She eventually had so many of them that she could nearly make up a map of her entire body using the scans that had been taken over the years. It was impressive.

Growing up, Chantal was always known as 'the encourager'. Even when she was going through her own troubles, she learnt to put other people ahead of herself and, as a result, she was able to rise above her own circumstances. She focused on people who were in need and who required prayer or encouragement. She now has a group on Facebook (called 'Inspired'), where she posts encouraging messages and life lessons for her viewers.

No matter what opposition was thrown at her, Chantal trusted in God one hundred per cent. When He closed relationship doors in her life, she trusted Him to open others. When surgeries were approaching, she trusted Him that everything would be successful. When she lost someone important to her, she trusted that He would be her comfort during the grief. When pain afflicted her body, she trusted Him to heal her; and if she didn't receive immediate healing, she trusted that He would give her the strength to endure.

Chantal always knew that God was faithful, and that He had a great future for her. She now wants to encourage you, her readers, that the best thing to do in any storm is to maintain your faith and hope in God. She wants to help you draw closer to God and then watch as He draws closer to you.